WILLIAM GOLDING

A CRITICAL STUDY

WILLIAM GOLDING
A CRITICAL STUDY

Usha George

ATLANTIC
PUBLISHERS & DISTRIBUTORS (P) LTD

Published by

ATLANTIC

PUBLISHERS & DISTRIBUTORS (P) LTD

7/22, Ansari Road, Darya Ganj,
New Delhi-110002
Phones : 23273880, 23275880, 23280451
Fax : +91-11-23285873
Web : www.atlanticbooks.com
E-mail : info@atlanticbooks.com

Branch Office
5, Nallathambi Street, Wallajah Road,
Chennai-600002
Phones : +91-44-64611085, 32413319
E-mail : chennai@atlanticbooks.com

ISBN 978-81-269-1008-3

Printed in India at Nice Printing Press, A-33/3A, Site-IV, Industrial Area, Sahibabad, Ghaziabad, U.P.

Preface

This book is a systematic and scholarly attempt to present to the readers a comprehensive study of William Golding as a religious novelist different from his contemporaries. The book comprises four chapters and each chapter can be regarded as a separate critical enterprise which may be of interest in its own right to those interested in the novelist in particular—his novels, the literary influences, plots, theme, structure, language and style or in the chapters discussing the novels in depth as in chapters 2 and 3 with chapter 4 concentrating on William Golding as a religious novelist.

William Golding, who acquired a new stature as the Nobel Laureate of Literature in 1983, was variously hailed as a fabulist, anti-realist, philosophical novelist and anthropologist of the imagination. He moved into the hallowed precincts of fiction relatively late in life, to occupy a unique place defying classification and categorisation.

He stands apart from most other contemporary novelists in English by cutting himself loose from two centuries of tradition in the English novel when the realistic mode was paramount. His technique was to employ myth to drive home his point. He constructs a mythopoeia relevant to contemporary man, since he believes in the anthropological notion, that it is through myth that the imaginative substances of religious belief may be expressed, communicated and enhanced. Myth is, according to Golding, something which comes out from the root of things in the ancient sense of being the key to existence—the whole meaning of life and experience as a whole.

The myth of all his books is the fall of man, his expulsion from Paradise, erected wit and infected will. After nearly three decades of literary discussion it has become commonplace to describe Golding as a religious writer. He has taken upon himself the formidable task of arousing the religious impulse and restoring to the recalcitrant time—the spiritual dimension—which is the stuff of vital religious mythopoeia. He goes back behind our distracting modern clutter of physical impediments to search for basic truths that have been obscured by material progress. As a spiritual cosmologist in the sense, Golding asserts that his discourse has been prompted by events and experiences, judged to be of cosmic significance and giving access to way things ultimately are.

Basically his novels reveal that man produces evil as a bee produces honey. Depressing truths about man and his nature are presented. He analyses our condition in terms of Original Sin. These are books about the terrible disease of being human, their unaltering aim is to make man face the sad fact of his own cruelty and lust. What these all proclaim is the fixed conviction that man is a fallen being. He is gripped by Original Sin. His nature is sinful and his state perilous. This is an announcement that lacks novelty. But he contends what is trite is true and a truism can become more than a truism when it is a belief passionately held.

Golding makes use of the novel form as a fit vehicle to reveal the dark place of human heart, the reality of their moral conditions, when isolated individuals or small groups are pushed into extreme situations. His works are characterised by exploration of the "darkness of man's heart" by deep spiritual and ethical questions. His allegorical fiction makes broad use of allusions to classical literature, mythology and Christian symbolism. Although no distinct thread unites his novels and his technique varies, Golding principally deals with evil and emerges with what is being characterized as the dark optimism. He strongly believes that evil is inherent in man and puts the locus of all evil in the "will" of man.

The moral framework of his novels is conceived in terms of traditional Christian symbolism, insisting on the recognition of the truth of the orthodox Christian version of human depravity as depicted in the "Book of Genesis" of the Old Testament. The theological concept Golding has transmitted into mythological form, is known to us under the biblical term "idolatry". The effect of idolatry is that man isolates himself off from God. There is no salvation in man's distorted nature, until he recognises the delusions of his idols and abandons the claim that he is the master of reality. Divine affirmation of man should be preceded by divine negation, destruction of the monstrous image of the self. This is the pattern we find in his novels.

The book comprises a critical study of his novels—*Lord of the Flies* and *The Inheritors*, focusing attention on the *Lord of the Flies* as a carefully worked out allegory in which man is presented as a creature, unredeemably fallen from grace, insisting on the recognition of the truth of the orthodox Christian version of human depravity. It examines the essential nature of humanity—the heart of darkness.

The Inheritors also repeats the same message. This novel effectively illustrates his view that innocence, goodness and happiness were instinctive before Homo sapiens developed and with them developed an all destructive urge to evil. The study shows how the novel deals with man's spiritual fall and his evolutionary rise. The fable, mythic in impulse, consciously tries to construct a mythopoeia relevant to contemporary man.

Golding as a religious novelist attempts to bring into focus innocence and guilt, freedom and necessity, transcendence and immanence, good and evil. His novels may be termed as "moral-models"—as a critique of Christian understanding, discarding the supernatural dimensions of traditional belief and offering a phenomenological version of reality. He has given us new ways of imaging Christian doctrines and mythological enactments which are also, in an important sense, the modern equivalents of the archetypal stories in "Genesis". He finds in the past meanings which are relevant to the present and what is reformulated is recognisably the mainstream of Christian tradition through a spectrum of incidents and characters.

The book will be useful to the students and teachers of English literature, researchers in this field and all those interested in knowing about the literary genius of William Golding.

USHA GEORGE

Contents

Preface .... *v*

1. Introduction 1

2. *Lord of the Flies* 30

3. *The Inheritors* 76

4. Conclusion 123

Bibliography 146

Index 154

Introduction

1

After the Second World War each decade in Britain has witnessed an abrupt and startling change in the national ethos. There is no doubt that the Second World War was as terrible a fracture in the twentieth century experience as the First had been. Its impact on world history, human consciousness and artistic expression was far greater than that of the conflict of just twenty-five years before. By the war's end in 1945, many of the great European cities were gutted by bombing, large regions of the continent lay in ruins, industrial activity ceased, harvests went unreaped, all frontiers were unsettled and many of Europe's people were displaced. Shattered survivors and returning prisoners of war wandered in a landscape of senseless borders and broken regimes. Brief moments of happiness were instantly engulfed in horror about the past and the present and usually in grim foreboding about the future too. Disillusionment was the order of the day.

Worse to come were the unbelievable facts about the deportations, massacre and genocide that had occurred in Nazi concentration and extermination camps like Buchenwald and Aushchwitz began to emerge. The Nuremberg Trials of Nazi war crimes in 1946 revealed the apocalyptic scale of the final solution planned by the Third Reich. Six Million Jews had perished in a terrible "Holocaust." Millions more, Jewish and non Jewish, had been deported or used as slave labour. Nor was the conscience of the Allies clear. As a result of Anglo-American research into the atom and its power, the war ended with another, no less terrible holocaust, the dropping of the atomic weapons on the cities of Hiroshima and Nagasaki in August 1945, which led to the Japanese surrender.

Thus the end of the war was the beginning of the Atomic age; human beings now had the power of universal self-annihilation. New attitudes and values resulted from the effects of the war. The holocaust and the nuclear cloud dominated the sensibility of the period. As political tensions continued, the hot war turned into a cold one, the post-war into the non-peace, the mood of anxiety, horror and apocalyptic peril increased. Winston Churchill announced that an Iron Curtain had descended across Europe, from Stettin to the Adriatic. By 1947 the term "cold war" was coined. Europe was not only cut geographically, but ideologically spilt between the influence of two vast atomically weaponed superpowers, the United States and the Soviet Union. Each represented a fundamental twentieth-century ideology; democratic liberal capitalism and totalitarian communism. The "post-war world" was born, in a web of confrontations, crisis and conspiracies. This long stasis did not end until forty-five years later when Marxist ideology and its command economies collapsed, the Berlin wall came down, and the 'new world order' started, with its own changed and wounded illusions about future history.

Much of the progressive optimism that had fed the idea of modernity began to fail as the second half of the century turned into a grim stand-off; the human hopes and ideological utopias of the Thirties now appeared at best naïve illusions, at worst treacheries and betrayals. If Europe's capitals, economies and political systems lay in ruins, so did its intellectual, ideological, metaphysical and cultural values: its ideas of the self, the state, politics, history, art, good and evil. The modern liberal morality could no longer cope with the religious problem of the evil in man.

The physical effects it produced and continues to produce carry moral, social and spiritual implication which only now we are beginning to feel and most of which we are powerless to alter. Essentially what the Machine Age has meant in human terms is the by-passing of man's irrational, non-logical element.

Most of the changes that have taken place during the last hundred years or so are interrelation; they share a common causality. The growth of an urban industrial society, the decay of traditional religious fundamentalism, the dissemination of scientific method, moral uncertainty, technological advance, the artificial retreat to primitivism, the flourishing neuroses which facilitated the development of psychology and psychiatry, thermo-nuclear deterrents, the death wish, sexual frustration or hysteria: one pattern binds them all together. We are not sure how we are affected by the breakdown of rural culture; we cannot judge the long-term effects of city life. Things have moved too fast for us. Man's metabolism changes slowly by nature; and in a century it has had to adapt itself more than in the previous thirty thousand years.

The notion that Science could be made a substitute for religion is comforting, yet ultimately dangerous. Man is a creature for whom patterns are essential and when T.H. Huxley and his successors destroyed the absolute sanctity of traditional Christianity, what was more natural than that the iconoclasts should set up a new church? Reason was their sovereign god; it could solve all the problems of the universe. The soul was a fiction, emotions could be rationalized in terms of hormones. God was a Job's comforter created by man in his own narcissistic image.

The consequence of this strangely unilateral creed was grave and most human attempts to upset the balance of nature tend to be calamitous. What happened, in effect, was that the emotional, instinctive and irrational element of human nature was treated simply as if it did not exist. Logic stuck its labels on the universe and analogies from the natural sciences multiplied fast. Natural selection was used to justify social persecution; the notion of evolution became transformed into Wellsian social progression. The smug religious superiority of the early Victorian gave place to the smug scientific superiority of the early anthropologist. The universe was as tidy and as comprehensible, for a few years, as the Crystal palace. But this was for a few years only. Neurosis grew and proliferated alarmingly. Reason could stick new labels on the emotions, but it could neither argue nor legislate them out of existence. It would rationalize God by discussing religion in terms of personal psychology; but God remained. Reason could rationalize its own motives, but his logical inference normally rested on a solid bedrock of emotional prejudice.

To have a better understanding of Golding's works fully this introduction is indispensable. "His job," Golding once wrote of the novelist, "is to scrape the label off things, to take nothing for granted to show the irrational where it exists."[1] His novels demonstrate this process in action. Man, has distanced himself away from nature and from his own self. He is cushioned in smugness; he has become his own God. Nothing can touch him. Golding has made it his task to break down these false illusions: his creed is that of the Delphic Oracle, "Know yourself." He believes that the only hope for humanity is self-knowledge attained and practiced by the individual.

In an interview for **Books and Art** (March 1958), he has made it clear that the basic problem of modern humanity was that of "learning to live fearlessly with the natural chaos of existence, without forcing artificial patterns on it."[2] Writing about schoolboys, Neanderthalers and dead sailors appeared to him to be simple means of turning a light on contemporary human nature. He proclaimed himself moralist for whom the novel is a "fit vehicle for pressing upon fellow creatures the reality of their moral condition."[3]

In a reply to a literary magazine's questionnaire, **The Writer in his Age** Golding writes:

> I am very serious, I believe that man suffers from an appalling ignorance of his own nature. I produce my own view, in my belief that it may be something like the truth. I am fully engaged to the human dilemma but see it as far more fundamental than a complex of taxes and astronomy.[4]

The questionnaire raised that question of 'engagement': should the writer concern himself with the political and social questions of his time? Golding's answer was unequivocal: the job of the writer is to show man his image *subspecies aeternitatis*. It is thus not an engagement to the concerns of the moment but to what is basic in the human condition, and in the forms that this engagement has led Golding to create, that his uniqueness lies.

The sense of engagement with a modern history, perplexing, terrifying and apocalyptic was to become part of the new spirit that emerged over the years of war and uneasy peace in British fiction. The life of literature in the post-war years has been deeply touched by the cultural disarray. The writers became the perceiving consciousness of post-war Britain and fiction was sought as the best medium to keep track of the reality of their experience.

Robert Hewism in his study of wartime writing states that "the war was a depressing time...the next years were to be worse."[5] But the threatening, overwhelming, depressing nature of the war and the years that followed did not obliterate fiction. Instead, it provoked and challenged the contemporary imagination into particular and productive reshaping of narrative, contributing to a fairly successful period for the novel, and certainly a distinctive one.

A distinctive new generation did emerge in the English novel after 1945. Some of them who began their writing career before the war but significantly extended them afterwards were Lawrence Durell, Malcolm Lowry, Samuel Beckett, Graham Greene, Evelyn Waugh, Ivy Crompton-Burnett, George Orwell and William Cooper. The new generation was influenced by a changed social climate, which bred a new aesthetic climate, for the post-war period was an era of revived liberalism, a tone appropriate to a political time when totalitarianism had been a national enemy, a time when democratic institutions needed to be remade and when liberal anxiety and uncertainty about human nature itself was a logical consequence of the impact of the revelations of Buchenwald and Auschwitz.

The moral urgencies of post-war English culture generated a new use and value for the novel form. Fiction became the voice for times when new social groups and classes were seeking articulacy and this was part of the cultural power of early novels by Kingsley Amis, John Braine, Alan Sillitoe, John Wain, David Storey and others. It was their books that for many, came to represent the novel in the 1950's, but in practice the scene was vastly more various, with writers of a quite different temper, bringing a much more fabulous and speculative mode into post-war English fiction by Muriel Spark, William Golding, Iris Murdoch, Doris Lessing and Anthony Burgess. The temper of criticism, was interpreting their novels as a socio-moral form.

When the post-war British fiction was dominated in the early 60's by the neo-realism of Doris Lessing, Kingsley Amis, Anthony Powell and C.P. Snow, Golding's effort seemed unique. Samuel Hynes remarks: "...it is in this engagement to what is constant in man's nature and in the correlative belief that a writer can make valid generalizations about the whole meaning of life that Mr. Golding stands most apart from his time—he is a writer who has designs on us, a moralist in an immoralist age."[6]

While novelists such as Amis, Wain and Murdoch seemed to be describing parochial worlds of considerable limitations, Golding was writing bold visionary fables which claimed for themselves a universal applicability.

William Golding, who acquired a new stature as the Nobel Laureate of Literature in 1983, was born in Cornwall on 19th of September 1911. He has spoken of how he was born into a world of "sanity and logic and fascination"[7] to employ his own words. He seems to have possessed a sense of perpetual wonder when he was young. He writes in *The Brass Butterfly*, "My life is passed in a condition of ravished astonishment."[8] He was against rational humanism. In an interview with James R. Baker conducted on July 5, 1981 at Golding's residence near Salisbury, England he discusses in detail the formative stage of his life.[9]

Dealing with the sense of protest he displayed against his father, he says that he thought that his father himself was less rigid than he seemed to be in his rational attitude. But he confesses that he did feel himself to be in a sort of rational atmosphere against which he kicked.

Golding experienced two things that he counts the greatest influences on his writing—first, the war and his service in the navy and second, his learning ancient Greek. The former confirmed for him the process, begun with the sinking of the Titanic, of shattering the liberal and optimistic image of man. The latter had large effects on his style. He feels a kinship with the world of Greeks and the ancient Egyptians. His faith in ancient life must have contributed much to the classic-revolt against rationalist humanist point of view. The Greek influences brought the element of the dynamic, concrete and enduring element to his fiction. His fiction goes deep to explore a philosophy of life instead of a superficial attempt to deal with the problem of Good and Evil. He did not relish the scientific humanism of writers like H.G. Wells and Gissing. The War and Greek literature together perhaps confirmed the dissociation from current and ephemeral affairs which makes Golding say that if the novelist "has a serious and Aeschylean, preoccupation with the human tragedy...he is committed to looking for the root of the disease instead of describing the symptoms."[10] Many of these influences can be traced on the embryonic mind which grew into that of a mature artist later.

Variously hailed as a fabulist, anti-realist, philosophical novelist and anthropologist of the imagination, William Golding who moved into the hallowed precincts of fiction relatively late in life, has come to occupy a unique place defying classification and categorization.

Golding's works lie before us as a systematic body of writing: written over four decades, characteristic yet flexible, various, changeable, open to new initiatives yet with a recognizable coherence. His first two novels *Lord of the Flies* (1954) and *The Inheritors* (1955) are carefully worked out allegories in which man is presented as a creature unredeemably fallen from grace. His best known novel *Lord of the Flies* describes the apparently inevitable degeneration into murderous savagery of a party of "decent" English school boys, marooned after an airplane crash, without adult control on a Pacific island. The result is a deliberate rebuttal of the optimistic assumption underlying Ballantyne's *The Coral Island*. Their attempts to organize their own society brings out the cruelties, jealousies, fears and hatred characteristic of primitive tribes and also a civilized community where they appear in a more complex form. This novel about the ascendancy in man of the powers of darkness can be read variously as a political, psychological or religious fable.

His next novel *The Inheritors* repeats the message of *Lord of the Flies*. It is a moving and brilliant *tour-de-force*, inhabiting the near-animal consciousness of Lok, a Neanderthal man and describing in his clumsy terms and with great pathos the casual destruction of his species by *Homosapiens*. This novel most effectively illustrate his view that innocence, good and happiness were instinctive before *Homosapiens* developed and with him an all destructive urge to evil. The reader is shown his ancestors, already armed, arrogant, murderous and corrupt—not superior to the Neanderthalers, only more clever and more evil. The most impressive feature about this novel is Golding's ability to enter into the consciousness of Neanderthal man, his dependence on the senses, his curiosity about the new people, his innocence until, like Adam and Eve, he learns the difference between good and evil. This novel also is primarily concerned with man's spiritual fall and his evolutionary rise. We are meant to see in Lok, the bemused innocent Adam before the Fall. The novel calls into question precisely what is it we have inherited, and suggests that principal among our legacies is guilt. This is an issue which is central to both his third and fourth novel *Pincher Martin* (1956) and *Free Fall* (1959) respectively. *Pincher Martin* is also a book set on an island and one that is concerned with survival and isolation, a perennial Golding theme. *Pincher Martin* parodies the Genesis myth of creation. A British Naval Officer and former actor by name Pincher Martin is blown off the bridge of a destroyer by a torpedo.

The novel tells of his courageous and ingenious struggle to preserve his life and to live until he is rescued. Our knowledge of his previous life is revealed through a series of flash-backs, the novel's dominant structural device is this alternation between past and present; between the contemporary world and the rock. Our admiration of Martin's epic fight for life is slowly undermined by our increasing knowledge of his viciousness and greed. The truth is that he is already drowned, his long battle for life on the rock was a fantasy sustained by his will, a 'ravenous ego' self-imposed purgatory, a frantic refusal to "die into heaven."

Golding's interest in the process of creation itself, which marks him as a contemporary writer, is further developed in the use of the painter Samuel Mountjoy, the protagonist of his next novel, *Free Fall.* While previously Golding has been interested in isolation, in depicting groups and individuals struggling for survival; in the past, and even in a world of his characters own making, now he portrays an individual in the contemporary world. The title suggests the religious connotations, the theological fall of humanity and it is possible that the title has been taken from Milton's epic poem *Paradise Lost* ("Sufficient to have stood: But free to fall"). It is largely a "stream of consciousness" in which Sammy Mountjoy looks back on his life in an effort to find out at what point he had lost his freedom of choice and action. It is a more optimistic book which posits both free will and the possibility of grace.

After the contemporary social realism of *Free Fall*, *The Spire* (1964) marks a clear return to the territory of primitive isolation which had characterized Golding's fiction up to that point, but this novel is also unlike any of its predecessors in one significant way, *The Spire* is the first of his books to use no literary analogue, although some critics have argued that Ibsen's play, *The Master Builder* lies behind the novel. The novel is based on the actual building of the spire of Salisbury Cathedral in the fourteenth-century. For the first time in Golding's work, the narrative is based on historical facts rather than on earlier fiction. Jocelin instructed by God, forces his spire upwards, at the cost of friendship and health, at the cost of other men's lives, at the cost of sacrilege. And when it is completed, he is dying, he no longer knows whether the work is blessed or damned, scared or obscene, only that the spire is there. It shows man apparently achieving something that is good. Yet everything connected with it is evil. Before he dies he reflects, that there is no innocent work and this is the truth of the book.

The Spire both integrates and develops the concerns of its predecessors, and yet it is also prophetic, anticipating several principal concerns of Golding's second phase as a novelist, notably the relationship of language to reality and the ambivalent nature of human experience.

Change and stasis are at the centre of *The Pyramid* (1967) the only novel Golding published during this phase of his career. It is a novel in three episodes about the life during 1930s in "Stilbourne" a small town near Salisbury. The title refers to the pyramid on which the inhabitants of a Wiltshire town climb and fall. Allegorically the novel resumes the themes of free will and the conflict between science and art that have always occupied Golding. The novel emphasizes the brutally destructive effects of the English class system.

The chronology of the novels published in the last fourteen years of his life were *Darkness Visible* (1979), *Rites of Passage* (1980), *The Paper Men* (1984), *Close Quarters* (1987), and *Fire Down Below* (1989). The second, fourth and fifth of these novels form a trilogy either known as *The Sea Trilogy,* or by the title given to the trilogy when it was published in a single volume in 1991: *To the Ends of the Earth.*

Rites of Passage which won the prestigious Booker Prize, can be read as a Buildungsroman (a novel of general education), just as *Free Fall* can be seen as a Kunstlerroman. This novel extends Golding's bleak view that innocence invites its own destruction. It is possible that it was actual death of a person that prompted him to write *Rites of Passage.* How can any of us ever know what another human being is experiencing? Even if we could know, how could we communicate our knowledge? are the questions which *Rites of Passage* attempts to answer. One of this most polished and articulate novels, paradoxically describes the inability of art, any art, adequately to represent, reality. He was awarded the Booker Mc Connell Prize for this.

Close Quarters, as the title implies has a claustrophobic atmosphere, as the world begins to shrink to the confines of the ship. The novel's concerns are specifically focused and it is structured around a few key incidents. It is a novel of over-compensation, of excess: mistakes Talbot makes in *Rites of*

Passage are rectified without moderation, resulting in further mistakes within *Close Quarters.*

Fire Down Below brings the trilogy to its conclusion. It shares many of the same interests as the previous two novels. The power of language continues to remain as the main theme. Innumerable circumstances conspire to convince the reader that nothing is necessarily as it appears—implies that appearance can be deceptive.

In his last novel, as he had done through all his writings, Golding contrasts the rational with the spiritual and echoes of the spiritual resonate throughout the closing pages of the novel, haunting its hero with visions of what he has lost.

By the late 1970's it was generally felt that Golding was a spent force, that he had taken his unique vision as far as it could go. *Darkness Visible* published in 1979, which won the James Tait Black Memorial Prize demonstrated that he still was one of the most extraordinary voices in contemporary literature. The book was received enthusiastically but with some bewilderment. The author did nothing to clear up the confusion by his refusal to speak about the novel at all. This quite uncharacteristic reticence on his part has contributed a great deal to the mystique which still surrounds the novel.

Darkness Visible is divided into three sections, each one of which is centred upon a specific character. The first section focuses upon Matty, who has emerged from the blazing ruins of London's docks after a bombing raid during World War II; and who acts throughout the novel like an Old Testament prophet. Matty tends to be seen as a figure representing "Good." The second section centres upon Sophy who, because of her criminal behaviour, sexual excess, and general attitude to life, tends to be seen as the anthithesis of Matty, and therefore as a figure representing 'Evil.' The third section describes the coming together of these two characters.

Most critics have reviewed this novel as Golding's condition of England novel; and the title is assumed to be taken from Milton's *Paradise Lost.* "No light, but rather darkness visible/ Served only to discover sighs of woe" (Bk. I, 11, 63-44), where

Milton describes Hell, as Satan surveys his new Kingdom after being expelled with all his warriors from Heaven. This leads to the inevitable assumption that would portray modern England as a kind of hell.

Golding's literary career has more than one universal feature: his late start as a publishing author. In an interview he has stated: "I had been writing ever since I was seven. I suppose you can say I've been effectively writing since I was thirty-five."[11] The rapidity with which he emerged as a major force is to be reckoned with in contemporary literature; the phenomenal success of his very first novel, *The Long Silence*, and the appearance of three more novels in six years—all this adds up to a creative record hard to parallel, and probably unique.

He stands apart from most other contemporary novelists in Britain, by cutting himself loose from two centuries of tradition in the English novel: centuries during which the realistic mode has been paramount. Golding made it clear that he was interested in a different kind of narrative-variously referred to as fable, allegory and myth.

J.R. Baker remarks, as a "product of wartime disillusionment, Golding retreated from modern problems to the art of allegory"[12], and Anthony Burgess described Golding as a "baroque bearded mythic visionary frowning at some terrible landscape of the mind."[13] The writer's technique is to employ myth to drive home his point. Golding constructs a mythopoeia relevant to contemporary man since he agrees generally with the anthropological notion that it is through myth that the imaginative substance of religious belief, is expressed, communicated and enhanced.

Fable has also been applied as a term to Golding's fiction. He writes "with all its drawbacks and difficulties, it was this method of presenting the truth as I saw it in fable form which I adopted for the first of my novels."[14] He remarked, "The fabulist is didactic, desires to inculcate a moral lesson,"[15] though the dramatic situation is primary, unlike in a parable, where the moral image is primary. The dramatic situation serves as an analogue of the world at large.

But in an interview with Frank Kermode back in 1959, he commented that he would prefer to have his novels considered as myth rather than fables.

> ...I think a myth is a much profounder and more significant thing than a fable. I do feel fable as being an invented thing on the surface, whereas myth is something which comes out from the root of things in the ancient sense of being the key to existence, the whole meaning of life and experience as a whole.[16]

This term may be made to describe both a superior mode of perception akin to Coleridge's Secondary Imagination which dissolves, diffuses, dissipates in order to recreate and to indicate an aesthetic landscape where the unchangeable patterns of human nature may be celebrated. Golding would agree with Aristotle's perception that the fundamental myth is the dramatic human tale and the myth of all his books as Frank Kermode has said is "The Fall of Man, the expulsion from Paradise, erected wit and infected will."[17] But Golding is not so much interested in myth as an aesthetic device, a distinct fictional form or mode but rather in myth-making and myth-responding proclivity of the human imagination. Myth is simply an imaginative tendency or mode of perception to which all art struggle. Thus, this is central to his type of religious vision. Myth carries its own powerful imaginative reasoning, ambiguities, religious overtones, adaptations and modulations, wrapped up within itself. Its power and meaning ultimately reside in and derive from the expectations people have of it.

Though Golding has called his books both *myths* and *fables* and both terms do point to a quality in the novels, it is necessary to recognize, that they are unusually tight, conceptualized, analogical expressions of moral ideas. Neither term is quite satisfactory, because both imply a degree of abstraction and an element of the legendary that Golding's novels do not have, and it seems better to call them simply *novels* which have certain formal properties that distinguish them from most current fiction.

The most striking of these properties is that Golding so patterns his narrative action as to make them images of ideas that is to say, it carries meanings apart from the meanings implied by character or those stated more or less didactically by the author. In all his books he has suggested a shape in the Universe that may, as it were, account for things. To direct the attention of his readers to that shape, Golding has chosen situations that violate what is basic and avoid both the merely topical and the subjective existence of the author. Almost all of his novels employ a situation that is remote in time or space, characters who are radically unlike the author and a narrative tone that is removed, analytical and judicial. Hence we must look for human relevance, to the patterned action itself; if we "identify" it must be with the moral—with the conception of man and the shape of the universe and not with this character or that one.

What these kinds of narrative have in common is a pre-occupation with something that lies beyond that representation or initiation of individual and social realities which has been the subject of novelists from Daniel Defoe to Evelyn Waugh. Golding's concern is with larger, more fundamental and abstract issues that may be called metaphysical to theological. Such works ask not "How does man live?" but "What manner of creature is man?" This kind of fiction has celebrated precedents in English—Bunyan's *Pilgrim's Progress,* Swift's *Gulliver's Travels,* Orwell's *Animal Farm,* Spenser's *Fairie Queen* and Milton's *Paradise Lost.* But since the eighteenth-century it has been lain at a distance from the main stream of fictional tradition. Golding's achievement has been to revalidate this alternative tradition for the modern world.

Golding makes no secret of his sources. Whatever terminology we use,—'debts,' 'borrowings,' 'parallels,' 'influence,' or 'sources'—it is important to recognize that what Golding does is to make a *creative* use of the great variety of sources. *Lord of the Flies* quickly announces itself as belonging to the sub-genre of science fiction which looks into the future and is most widely associated with H.G. Wells. But a more significant relationship is to R.M. Ballantyne's juvenile novel, *The Coral Island* (1857) to which he has made an explicit reference in the last page of his own.

Golding himself has declared that "one book never comes out of another, and *The Coral Island* is not *Lord of the Flies*".... One work does not come from another unless it is still-born."[18] Golding's novels can be described as "reactive experiments."[19] His *Lord of the Flies* is not *The Coral Island*. But allows Ballantyne's optimistic tale of survival and self-discipline to stand for a whole set of beliefs and attitudes that he sets about contradicting and demolishing. This bold contrastive, even schematic method is the essence of Golding's art. Other novels which have been identified as parallels to this particular novel are *The Swiss Family Robinson* (1813) by Johann Rudolf Wyss, a Swiss author; Defoe's *Robinson Crusoe* (1719) (contrastive or 'reactive' since Crusoe's thirty-year preservation of his reason and piety is a far cry from the rapid moral deterioration of the modern school boys). Several reviewers have compared it with Richard Hughe's *A High Wind in Jamaica* (1929), though Golding has stated that he did not read Hughe's book until after he had written his novel; and the phrase "the darkness of man's heart" a few lines from the end of *Lord of the Flies* appear to be an allusion to Conrad's *Heart of Darkness* (1899). It is tempting to follow up the resemblance by suggesting that the pig's head in Golding's novel may owe something to those decapitated heads on stakes that Conrad's Marlow finds when he reached Kurtz's settlement in the heart of Africa. But Golding has stated in an interview that he had "never read"[20] Conrad's story.

Golding uses Wells in his second novel, *The Inheritors* as he had used Ballantyne in his first; as a point of departure, a convenient representative of a set of views—optimistic, confident, progressive that his fiction tries to expose as hollow. The influence works by contraries. Wells, the heir of Darwin, views evolution as a process of improvement, a development from lower to higher states in the moral as well as the intellectual and physical spheres; Golding questions this whole assumption, since the New Men who drive out the innocent Neanderthals are capable of evil.

Pincher Martin, appears to be a novel of the present day or the immediate past, and evidently draws on the author's own wartime experience, but it actually turns out to refer to the timeless state of existence after death. A most striking source or parallel exposed regarding this novel is to the all but forgotten book with virtually the same title: *Pincher Martin*, O.D., *A Story of the Inner Life of the Royal Navy* (1916), by Commander Taprell Dorling, who used the pseudonym 'Taffrail.' Golding has denied owning anything to it but the title. Unconscious memory may have played a part, since, J.S. Ryan, who has made a comparison of the two novels suggests that "the dependence of the one on the other is considerable...almost every person and action in the Golding novel can be found to have a parallel or antithesis in the earlier novel."[21] The phrase 'inner life' in Taffrial's subtitle is also taken up by Golding. *The Coral Island*, which includes an episode in which a pair of sea-boots are washed ashore, a poem "Rockall" by Michael Roberts, which contains the lines:

> The waves break on the bare rock, the traveller remembers/
> Shipwreck, the struggle with the water, the wild climb....

That Golding had Rockall in mind as the apparent site of Martin's ordeal is confused by a punning reference to it in the novel. Another reference is made to the story "An occurrence at Owl Greek Bridge" by the American author Ambrose Bierce. Both make use of the same abrupt concluding reversal for which Golding has so often been praised or blamed for. The hero, whose escape and return home has been narrated, is found to have died at an early stage of the story.

Peter Green has called *Pincher Martin* 'Aeschylean'[22] recognising the similarity of situation between Golding's protagonist and that of Aeschylus's *Prometheus Bound*. The relationship is a "reactive" one, since whereas Aeschylus's hero is persuaded to submission, Golding's like that of Shelly's *Prometheus Unbound* refuses to submit. Gabriel Josipovici has suggested that it is a logical sequel to *The Inheritors*. Golding's intention in *Pincher Martin* is to "isolate one of the new men, the 'inheritors', and then to explore what man is like—not what he thinks he is like, but what, stripped of the protective clothing of civilization, he really is."[23] The notion of isolation readily brings to mind Defoe's archetypal hero—but Martin tries to "tame" the rock and reduce its starkness to a semblance of the civilized world, as Crusoe does with his much more hospitable and amendable island; his attempt is doomed to failure, as Crusoe's is not.

The influences referred to may sometimes be unconscious. Golding has stated in an interview "that if people engage in writing about humanity, they're likely in certain circumstances to see something of the samething.[24] His novels are not "researched" in any systematic ways: he writes about the things he knows and understands, and sometimes that knowledge and understanding have been furnished by his reading.

However, there remains one important literary influence, general and pervasive rather than specific and localized; that of the drama, especially Greek tragedy and Shakespeare. In an interview, Golding states:

> I was more or less brought up on Shakespeare and that has an influence...there's no doubt that I know my Shakespeare pretty well by heart.... I don't think my novels come out of novels. If they owe anything to previous work, and obviously they must, it's the theatre much more than novel writing. It's great drama in particular. I think of the shape of a novel, when I do think of a novel as having a shape, as having shape precisely like Greek drama....[25]

If the 'shape' of Greek tragedy helps to determine the structure of his novel and to account, for his fondness for such devices as 'discovery' (anagnoris) and 'reversal' (peripeteia) the language of Shakespeare's plays must be seen as influencing the extraordinarily, rich, dense and complex prose of his novels.

When discussing some of war's effects on fiction in *The Novel Now* Anthony Burgess quotes Jean Paul Sartre's view that

> ...we have been taught to take Evil seriously.... Dachau and Auschwitz have...demonstrated to us that Evil is not an appearance, that knowing its cause does not dispel it, that it is not opposed to God as a confused idea is to a clear one.[26]

War stimulated novelists fairly immediately to examine the nature and relation of good and evil, innocence and experience,

God and Devil. Burgess's quotation and the various examples of Hughes, Thomas and Fielding suggest that such concerns are extended into later decades by the sustained challenge of the concentration camp's memory; the developing legacy of the war's impact on imagination. Golding provides a figuration of these continuing interests in recent fiction and of their likely wartime origins, in his opening to *Darkness Visible* (1979) which depicts an innocent child, Matty, walking out of the Fiery centre of war in the London City, as if "born from the sheer agony of a burning city."[27] One half of his face is light the other turned dark. The novel shows him going on to enter a strange "universal struggle" between powers of good and evil, half-spiritual, half-earthly. This scene is emblematic of not the source but the nature of moral concerns which have remained fairly constant ever since his first novel.

He actively opposed the behaviourist assumption that human ills are related to the environment and put the locus of all evil in the "will" of man. He told Owen Webster that "evil enters the world through humanity and through no other creature"[28] and his fictions have sustained an enquiry into that dark premise or conviction, the equation of intelligence with evil. His novels take a radical view of the human condition and emphasis evil, egotism and guilt.

Golding living the horrors of Belsen Buchenwald cannot hold any radiant view of man's nature. It is the darkness of the night that envelops and even penetrates his perspective. A major part of the personal perspective of Golding is clear from his remark: "There were things done during that period from which I shall have to avert my mind lest I should be physically sick. They were not done by the head hunters of the New Guinea or by some primitive tribe in the Amazon. They were done skillfully coldly by educated men, doctors, lawyers, by men with tradition of civilization behind them, to beings of their own kind."[29]

The war was fought on the proverbial saying that everything is fair in love and war. No wonder, he reacted violently to the horrors of the Concentration camps. Walter Allan remarks of

Golding's fiction: "...great gifts of imagination and narrative ...force us to accept, as part of the truth about man and his nature, the realities summoned up in our time in the hysterical nastiness of Nazism and Concentration camps."[30]

Man's propensity towards evil, Golding argues is man's real nature, yet it was ignored and hidden by those who urged man's perfectibility and pictures his steady climb of the evolutionary ladder towards "sweetness and light."[31] He has no illusions about man's progression. His novels focus attention on the regression. They are solely interested in moral values such as innocence and his morally depressed state wherein he falls a prey to guilt, evil and violence, free will and responsibility. Golding wrote without mincing matters, "I believe that man was sick not exceptional man but average man. I believe that the condition of man was that of a morally deceased creation."[32] Fleck comments on such an attitude of Golding in terms of theology. He says, "in theological terms, his pessimistic view of humanity's inherent imperfection is familiar as the Fall of Man, that vast aboriginal calamity, to use the phrase of Newman, which shares man's soul. Golding's view is that each and everyone of us is a morally flawed creature."[33]

So however heterodox his fictional topographies may be, his seminal themes, like those other obsessional artists are limited and homogenous. There has been an underlying consistency of purpose, a sense that all these novels are part of a single-minded exploration and exposition of the nature of good and evil. Each of Golding's novels represents another face carved from his earliest, most deeply held conviction that the two signs of man are his belief in God and his capacity to kill. For Golding remarks:

> It is not too much to say that man invented war at the very earliest moment possible. It is not too much to say that as soon as he could leave a sign of anything he left a sign of his belief in God.[34]

He has remarked, "I cannot *not* believe in God" and warily continued:

> My guess is that there are infinite cosmoses...and beyond that is the thing I call the Good. It seems to me that there

> could be infinite modes of life, and that they would all be sustained by the beings that inhabit them. In other words, we have invented our own universe. We have discovered that there are black holes in here and then discovered that out there.... May be there are universes of awful suffering, may be there are universes of awful pleasure, but I guess that beyond them there must be a Good which is Absolute.... So when you ask me if I believe in God, it's not even a matter of what I believe. Its what I suspect.[35]

To provide accounts of religious belief is one thing; to convince us of their urgency at their centrality is quite another. Golding has taken upon himself the formidable task of arousing the religious impulse and restoring to the recalcitrant time the spiritual dimension which is the stuff of vital religious mythopoeia.

After nearly three decades of literary discussion it has become common place to describe him as a religious writer. He has called himself an incompetently "religious" man and his works certainly seem to concern themselves with man's religious self, in the widest sense of his vision of a relationship with something outside himself—"I've never been able to believe in myself, I believe in God, I don't believe in myself, I believe in God.... The real point is that, if you believe in God, you can envisage your complete extinction with great cheerfulness because it is enough for God to exist.[36]

He denounces the complacency of the modern man who has "an easy answer to all problems simply because they have never looked further than the rashes appearing on the skin."[37] He is not content with the superficial but desires to look into things. In his probe, he is a religious novelist, in the sense that unlike much contemporary British writers, his primary and penetrative concern is with what is perennial in the human condition. He looks not simply for the relationship of man and man, but the relationship of man, the individual to the Universe and through the cosmic situation to God.

His fiction plays with the puzzle of Proverbs 23:18 that "Where there is no vision, the people perish." This is, in the widest sense, a religious exploration and without stating so explicitly, all the fiction embodies this diction for it deals with the primordial pattern of human experience. His central theme is pre-occupied with what is permanent in man's nature—his evil in *Lord of the Flies,* his origins in *The Inheritors,* his destiny in *Pincher Martin* his guilt in *Free Fall,* his vision in *The Spire*, his heart's meaningness in *The Pyramid* and heady inventions in *The Scorpion God.*

Golding's theology bring into focus—innocence and guilt, freedom and necessity, transcendence and immanence, good and evil. He describes realities of human behaviour and consciousness which theological statements indicate but do not enact: "What is it like to experience the fall from innocence into sin? What is it like to experience damnation? To create an idolatrous God in the image of man or beast? To be stretched on the rack of such contraries as life and death, sacred and profane love, the self and the other.... And what would it be like to experience atonement and resurrection."[38] These are some of the themes of his novels, the stuff of existence upon which theological reflection operates.

He goes back behind our distracting modern clutter of physical impediments to search for the basic truths that have been obscured by material progress. He is a spiritual cosmologist. In an interview Golding remarks: "We understand that we are not only mysterious in ourselves but in a situation of bounded mystery. It's a controlling fact in my life and in what I write.[39] In Golding's view "contemporary man lacks vision. How is he not to perish.[40] In each of his novels, there is the effort of bridge building between the physical world which contemporary man accepts and the spiritual world which he ignores. In a century of disbelief and formidable violence, Golding's mythopoeia contends, mystery is experienced only as malignancy not as holiness or weakness. It is as though the spiritual is experienced not as individual or transcendent mercy, but as personal and universal guilt. Man, according to Golding, abstracts from his violence, something his nature possesses and projects it as fear of a demon which will destroy him, thus the central symbol for the spiritual dimension is "darkness"[41] and the central symbolic episode involves the nightmare world where character undergoes atavistic re-ordering or, as in the case of Pincher Martin death itself. His total vision in his novels is a close approximation to Christian Symbolism to communicate the Ultimate Reality.

It is easy to perceive that their symbolism is, in essence, theological. Both *Lord of the Flies* and *The Inheritors* are concerned with the primal loss of innocence. *The Inheritors* can be read as an anthropological allegory of the Fall, with Lok and Fa as a prelapsarean Adam and Eve. *Pincher Martin* as the last chapter proves, explicitly concerns the sufferings of a dead man who has created his own purgatory.

It is a moral axiom of Golding that Man, and Man alone, introduced evil into the world: a view which is hardly separable from the doctrine of Original Sin. This is suggestive. The sin of Adam, Eve and Cain is what we see in today's man. He represents himself, theologically, as what used to be loosely termed a Deist; and yet the moral framework of his novels is conceived in terms of traditional Christian symbolism.

The theological concept Golding has transmitted into mythological form is known to us under the biblical term *idolatry*. The meaning of this term is analysed in Ezekial 14: 1-14 and Romans 1:18-27 as follows:

1. Men take their idols into their hearts. The meaning of an idol is the meaning man gives to it. The idolator constructs an objective counterpart of his desires with the purpose of legitimatizing them and enabling him to their free rein uncontrolled by conscience. The gods of the idolator are projections that mould reality nearer to the heart's desire.
2. Men put the stumbling block of their iniquity before their faces. Idol worship thus comes to be associated with violent physical stimulus, sexual excess and perversion, cruelty, violence, human sacrifice and so forth. All this is a product of the disturbed psyche of the modern man, but it is cast on to a demonic reality which makes it far more terrible and destructive.
3. The effect of idolatry is that men cut themselves off from God and no longer hear the divine word. That word is

not an echo of human ambition: it is a critique, a judgment of man's moral destruction. God summons men to depart from iniquity and to align themselves with divine will.

4. But man's false beliefs must be shattered. He must be brought into the cosmic night before the true light can shine upon him. There is no salvation in man's distorted nature. God comes to that nature as a "consuming fire" (Hebrew, 12:29). Yet when men do seek the Lord, they find in him a reality beyond their dreaming.

The idea of God's negation of man constantly recurs in Christian thought. Man cannot receive divine grace until he recognizes the delusiveness of his idols and abandons the claim that he is master of reality. The divine affirmation of man is preceded by divine negation, by destruction of the monstrous image of himself which he projects upon the Universe. This is a pattern which we find in Golding's novels.

To portray his notions about the mysterious and multiple modes of spiritual life in concrete novelistic terms, Golding has devised an ingenious narrative form termed as the ideographic structure by Virginia Tiger. The term ideographic, is used to describe Golding's apparently intentional use of a specific and unusual structural form to make an essentially religious, though not necessarily Christian statement in an historical time when such statement cannot be made explicitly. It consists of two narrative movements, the second of which is a coda. This structure also involves two different perspectives on the same situation: that emerging from the first movement and that emerging from the coda. In the first narrative movement events are seen from one character's point of view, while in the coda events are seen either from another character's point of view or from the enlightened consciousness of the novelist's protagonist. The ideographic structure moves the reader outside the world of sensation he has been inhabiting and puts him abruptly into another world of sensation.

The ideographic structure seems to create two contradictory perspectives on the same circumstances since the coda reverses the expectations which the first movement has built up. Though superficially contradictory, the two perspectives can be linked by the reader. Finally in forcing the reader to build the bridge between contradictory perspectives, this kind of a structure forces the reader to accept paradoxes of existence which the novel's characters are presented as being unable to perceive or accept. The bridge between the two is to be built by the reader who is driven by the paradoxical structure of each novel to accept paradoxes of existence, which are to Golding symptoms of the spiritual world.

An intense awareness of the physical world is accompanied at every point by an awareness of metaphysical world. Golding's imagination is always on the move, constantly seeing in detail a hint of larger design. "The form and structure of his work are designed to concentrate the eye on that larger design, but paradoxically, it is through the concentration on the detail that we become fully aware of the whole."[42]

The forms that Golding uses carry implications both for the kind of action selected and for the kind of characters involved on it. Since Golding proposes to embody general truths, he is committed to select those human experiences that can be viewed as *exemplary* and not merely *typical.* The event also bears its share of the patterned meaning. Consequently the novels tend on the whole to be short and densely textured, and the characters, function as exemplars of facets of man's nature.

He writes from clear and strong moral assumptions and these assumptions give form and direction to his fiction. Golding's novels might be termed as "moral models."[43] He accepts certain traditional ideas about man and his place in the world: that mind, by meditation and speculation, arrives at truth; it finds in the past, meanings which are relevant to the present and available through memory; it appropriately concerns itself with metaphysics and with morals. Though Golding is a moralist, he is not a moral-maker and his novels do not belong with Aesop's fables, but with important symbolic novels of our century, with Camus's and Kafka's.

Some maintain that a theological novelist compromises his integrity as an artist. He starts with some forgone conclusions which make impossible the free exercise of the creative imagination. For the Christian, truth has already been made manifest and there is nothing new to discover. So characters tend to become mere exemplars of doctrine, puppets, whose actions reinforce a message which exists independently of them. Thus a Christian writer is a polemicist.

But Golding's works do not fall under this condemnation. A Christian writer need not bow before a set of doctrinal absolutes. To deal with theology does not mean spinning abstract formulations of nonempirical reality out of one's head. His theology need indicate no more than an understanding of man which takes his experience of transcendence into account, which finds inadequate the positivist doctrine that the individual can be described in terms of the social and psychological structures in which he exists. To have a theology in this sense is to assert that man cannot be understood apart form his relationship to transcendent reality.

A tragic writer like Golding tends to explore the absence of God from the centre of consciousness. He tries to show what happens when man claims that reality is limited to the area of his own mastery, and he explores the demonism that grips man when they interpret reality in terms of their own greed and fear. He also wrestles with the baffling contraries. His theology brings into focus: transcendence and immanence, freedom and necessity, being and becoming, good and evil innocence and guilt. Finally he implies the harmonization of contraries in a divine act of reconciliation.

However remote and academic the theologian may seem, Golding asserts that his discourse has been prompted by events and experience judged to be of cosmic significance and giving access to the way things ultimately are. This process also operates in reverse, when the creative imagination reenacts in the form of myth, the immediate experience, pre-supposed by doctrinal formulation. It can also enact experience which brings theological statement under appraisal and challenges its assumptions. Events and new knowledge can cause a disorientation calling for new theological solutions. But how far a basic doctrine can be qualified and reinterpreted while remaining the same doctrine is a perplexing question today. To give a specific example, which brings us near the centre of Golding's concern, we may ask whether the traditional Christian doctrine of Original sin is still the same doctrine when its basis in the story of the Fall is recognized as myth not history, and when Original sin is interpreted not as the result of a primal rebellious act, but as an inevitable concomitant of man's existential condition. It can be said that the doctrine is no longer the same if it leaves God out—if, for instance, human wickedness and misery are attributed to prerational drives deriving from man's animal ancestry which in time he will outgrow. The Christian doctrine of Original sin is about the rupture of man's relationship with God, it is not about the incompleteness of evolutionary development. One factor that makes Golding a Christian writer is his recognition of the difference between these two anthropologies and his siding with the theological rather than the biological version though he also recognizes that the terms in the Christian doctrine which becomes existentially significant today will require a reformation of orthodoxy.

Although basic Christian doctrines may be held to be unchanging, what is more important is the ways they are stated, the extent to which their relevant to modern knowledge and awareness is displayed and the strength and range of their explanatory power. Thus the best way of dealing with theology is to do what Golding has done—that is, enact the kind of experience in which theological doctrines come to life and take in depth, so that they are lifted out of the context of arid academicism where they can be ignored.

Golding's success as a Christian writer depends not upon the degree to which he engages us in discussion of theological ideas, but upon the degree to which he shocks us into recognition of the forgotten elements in the recesses of our awareness.

Basically what his novels have to say is that "man produces evil as a bee produces honey."[44] Depressing truths about man and his nature are presented. He analyses "our condition in terms of Original sin." They are books about the "terrible diseases of human being," their unfaltering aim is to make man face "the sad fact of his own cruelty and lust."[45] What they all proclaim is the fixed conviction that "Man is a fallen being. He is gripped by Original sin. His nature is sinful and his state perilous." This is an announcement that lacks novelty. But he contends "what is trite is true and a truism can become more than a truism when it is a belief passionately held."[46]

Golding's novels of all contemporary writers of fiction reveal in the very grain of the imagination, his religious concern. That concern is quite different in Golding's case, from the way we might use the term to describe the work of Graham Greene or Mauriac or Heinrich Boll, all of whom have shown themselves at one time or another to be interested in religious themes. Such an interest is tangential in Golding; when we talk of Golding exercising a religious imagination we feel that the primary effort has been to make us feel, within this world, the overwhelming importance of a world elsewhere, a Creator elsewhere.

NOTES

1. Owen Webster, *Novelists in Interview* (John Haffenden, Metheun, London, New York, 1985), p. 97.
2. O. Harry Blamer, *Twentieth-Century Literature*, 2nd ed. (Macmillan, 1986), p. 223.
3. *Ibid.*
4. "The Writer in His Age," in a reply to a questionnaire, *London Magazine*, 10 (May 1959), pp. 45-46.
5. Robert Hewism, "The Cost of a Vision," *Times Literary Supplement,* 16 (April 1964), p. 310.
6. Samuel Hynes: *Moral Models: William Golding's Novels*; 1954-67 ed. (Norman Page, 1985), p. 100.
7. Stephen Metcalf, *William Golding: Writer and their Works* (Scotland: Longmans, 1975), p. 22.
8. William Golding, *Brass Butterfly: A Play in Three Acts* (London: Faber and Faber, 1958), p. 22.
9. James R. Baker, *Twentieth Century Literature: Golding Special Issue* (Summer 1982), p. 32.
10. "The Writer in His Age," *London Magazine*, 10 (May 1959), p. 46.

11. Jack I. Biles, *Talk: Conversations with William Golding* (New York: Harcourt), p. 15.
12. J.R. Baker, *William Golding: A Critical Study* (New York: St. Martin's Press, 1965), p. 17.
13. Anthony Burgess, "Golding Unbuttoned," *The Listener* (November 1964), p. 717.
14. Golding, *Fable: The Hot Gates*, p. 86.
15. *Ibid.*, p. 25.
16. Golding to Kermode in "The Meaning of it All," *Books and Bookmen* (August 1959), p. 10.
17. *Ibid.*, p. 15.
18. Bernard F. Dick, "The Novelist is a Displaced Person: A Interview with William Golding," *College English*, 26 (1965), p. 36.
19. Bernard S. Oldsey and Stanley Weintraub, *The Art of William Golding*, New York (Harcourt, 1965), p. 36.
20. James Keating, Interview with William Golding in James R. Baker and Arthur P. Ziegler. In eds. *William Golding's Lord of the Files*, Casebook ed. (New York: Putnam's, 1964), p. 194.
21. J.S. Ryan, "The Two Pincher Martin's: From Survival Adventure to Golding's myth of dying, *English Studies*, 45 (1974), p. 142.
22. Peter Green in his essay *The World of William Golding*, pp. 49-50 has suggested Bierce's story and Robert's poem as sources or Parallels.
23. Oldsey and Weintraub, op. cit., p. 116.
24. Keating, op. cit., pp. 194-95.
25. James R. Baker, "An Interview with William Golding," *Twentieth Century Literature*, 28 (1982), p. 161.
26. Anthony Burgess, *The Novel Now: A Student's Guide to Contemporary Fiction* (London: Faber and Faber, 1971), p. 184.
27. William Golding, *Darkness Visible*: 1979 Rpt. (London: Faber and Faber, 1980), p. 20.
28. Quoted from Owen Websters, *Novelists in Interview*, p. 97.
29. Golding, *The Hot Gates*, p. 87.
30. Walter Allan, *Tradition and Dream: The English and American Novel from the Twenties to Our Time* (London: Dent, 1964), p. 291.

31. A.D. Fleck, *The Golden Bough: Aspects of Myth and Ritual in Lord of the Flies* (London: J.M. Dent, 1971), p. 163.
32. Golding, *The Hot Gates*, p. 89.
33. A.D. Fleck, op. cit., p. 163.
34. Golding, "Before the Beginning," *The Spectator*, 28 (May 1961), p. 786.
35. Golding to John Haffenden, "An Interview," *Quarto Magazine*, p. 11.
36. John Haffenden, *Novelists in Interview* (London, New York: Mctheun, 1985), p. 111.
37. Peter Green, "The World of William Golding," *A Review of English Literature*, 2 (April 1996), pp. 62-63.
38. Jack I. Biles and Robert O. Evans, ed. *William Golding: Some Critical Considerations* (Lexington: University Press of Kentucky, 1979), p. 54.
39. Golding to John Haffenden, "William Golding: An Interview," *Quarto Magazine*, Vol. II, No. 2 (Nov. 10, 1980), p. 9.
40. Virginia Tiger, *The Dark Fields of Discovery* (London: Marian Bryans, 1975), p. 15.
41. *Ibid.*, pp. 15-16.
42. John Carey ed., *William Golding, The Man and His Books: A Tribute on his 75th Birthday* (London: Faber and Faber, 1986), p. 97.
43. Samuel Hynes, *Moral Models: William Golding's Novels*: 1954-67, ed. (Norman Page, 1985), p. 100.
44. Golding, *Fable: The Hot Gates*, p. 87.
45. Alastair Nixen, *Notes on Lord of the Flies* (Tengam York Press, 1980), p. 26.
46. Golding, *The Hot Gates*, p. 88.

Lord of the Flies

2

Never again will I put the earth under a curse because of what man does; I know that from the time he is young his thoughts are evil.

Genesis 8:20

In the words of Jesus in St. Mathew, 18:4, "The greatest in the kingdom of heaven is the one who humbled himself and becomes like this child," childhood is presented as a state of innocent goodness, a state which may be regarded as the kingdom of heaven on earth. As adults, fallen from this happy state, we may hanker after a return to it and the possibility of such a conversion is held out to us by Jesus in the Biblical passage, St. Mathew, 18:3, "I assure you that unless you change and become like children, you will never enter the Kingdom of Heaven." There is room for optimism about human nature of our Universe, for the speaker is the Creator and loving ruler of the Universe who came down to earth to suffer and die so that we might be redeemed or rescued from our wickedness and restored to the original purity and happiness as we see in children and remember as our experiences of childhood.

But we live in a cruel world which can only be governed by malevolent demons whose delight is to torture us. If we wish to see an image of these dark gods or devils we need to look no further than children or our childhood, need only examine the ghastly and ferocious play of children, where we see how little devils torture and kill insects for fun, playing God with flies. From within and without we are beset by evil-in our human nature there is a terrifying propensity towards wanton cruelty which is evident even in children. There are number of occasions in the Bible which highlights that every inclination of man's heart is evil from childhood. David confesses before the Lord in Psalm, 51:5, "I have been evil from the day I was born; from the time I was conceived I have been sinful."

One allegorical feature of Golding's *Lord of the Flies* (1954) a powerful first novel, written with style and authority, is that the innocence of the child is a crude fallacy, for *Homo-sapiens* have by nature a terrible potentiality for evil, which cannot be controlled and eradicated by any humane political system, no matter how respectable.

This novel enjoyed a modest initial success. Lionel calls it "One of the most striking literary phenomena of recent years and a book that seem to have captivated the imagination of a whole generation."[1] It is hard to think of another first novel that moves forward with such sureness and confidence. Part of the explanation, of course, is that it was not his first novel. Golding remarked in a television interview in 1959 that he spent "ten years, perhaps, learning to write by imitating other people and learning very late that, of course, I was merely writing other people's novels indeed of my own."[2] This novel, quickly became both a campus cult-book and an examination text and was filmed in 1963.

Lord of the Flies is first and foremost a gripping adventure story: "...it falls well within the main stream of several English literary traditions. It's a boys' book as are *Treasure Island*, *The Wind in the Willows*, *A High Wind in Jamaica* and other books primarily about juvenile characters which transcend juvenile appeal; it is in the tradition of the survival narrative, along with *Robinson Crusoe*, *The Swiss Family Robinson* and even Barrie's *Admirabel Crichton*."[3] In addition to being an adventure story, the novel has important dimensions, morally, psychologically and theologically.

It has been variously interpreted as religious, political, psychological and anthropological. In the essay "Fable", in *The Hot Gates* Golding avers that *Lord of the Flies* is a multilayered work and open to various interpretations."[4] The novel has been plausibly interpreted as a Christian Parallel and Greek tragedy and less plausibly with reference to neo-Freudian, Jungian, and Marxian concepts.[5]

James R. Baker and Bernard Dick conclude that the novel is an allegory on the disintegration of society due to a tragic flaw in human nature: man fails to recognize, and thereby appease, the irrational part of his soul. Howard Babb, argues that the "innocent pride" attributed to the boys is pride in their own wisdom.[6] As Jack says, "After all we're not savages, we're English and the English are best at everything" (p. 47).

E.L. Epstein believes that the Freudian psychoanalytic theory is relevant: "The Devil is not present in any traditional religious sense, Golding's Beelzebub is the modern equivalent, the anarchic amoral, driving force that Freudians call the Id."[7]

Viewed from another perspective, the novel becomes what some commentators call an anti-Utopian satire. For the island society is microcosmically a human society, related to the 'grown-up' society that occasioned the Original fall from the skies. Anthropologically the society is a mirror of the first primitive societies of prehistoric man; its progress illustrates a biological maxim: that the development of the individual recapitulates in capsule time the development of the species.[8] The tale can be viewed in social psychological terms to show how intelligence (Piggy) and common sense (Ralph) will always be overthrown in society by sadism (Roger) and the lure of totalitarianism (Jack). Seen in political terms it is a dramatization of 'the modern political nightmare'[9] in which responsible democracy is destroyed by charismatic authoritarianism.

Terms such as allegory, parable, fable, science fiction, romance have been variously suggested. Judging from his comments in the essay "Fable" Golding's own preference is the term fable, which he once defined as "allegory that has achieved passion."[10] Another persistent classification that has attended to the book's intellectual schemata is affinity to neither romance nor realism, its definition as neither parable nor fable, but its relation to the Christian apologia. Frederick Karl's discussion in *A Reader's Guide to the Contemporary English Novel*, was first to suggest that Golding wrote religious allegories whose conceptual machinery undermines the 'felt life' of the tale: "The idea…invariably is superior to the performance itself."[11]

This passage really sums up all the pertinent critical attitudes with regard to this text: "It is, in fact, a cannily constructed—perhaps contrived-allegory for a twentieth-century doctrine of Original sin and its social and political dynamics and it conforms essentially to a quite orthodox tradition not really more pessimistic than the Christian view of man."[12]

Reacting against the Romantic notion that man is basically noble, if freed from the fetters of society, Golding insists that evil is inherent in man; a terrifying force which he must recognise and control.

Golding's experiences in World War II provided him with a tremendous insight into human nature. He realised that everyone had within him the potential to be utterly brutal should circumstances demand it. His essay, 'Fable' provides a clear and interesting statement of the intellectual background which lay behind the novel. He remarked that before the World War II "I believed in the perfectability of social man, that a correct structure of society would produce goodwill, and that therefore you could remove all social ills by a reorganization of a society...but after the war, I did not because I was unable to. I had discovered what one man could do to another."[13] He realized how rational intelligence and material progress made man more corrupt, violent and destructive. Golding said, "World War II was a turning point for me. I began to see what people were capable of doing."[14] The impact of this realization was that this potential for greed, innate cruelty and selfishness lay within all of us, not just our war-time enemies, waiting only for circumstances suddenly to unleash it into a powerful manifestation. It was this observation that led Golding to investigate a theme common to all his novels: man's capacity for inhumanity to man and the point in time when man fell from the perfect state of innocence into which he was born.

Experience of war, as well as of such totalitarian regimes as Fascism and Stalinism made Golding realize that "man was sick-not exceptional man, but average man...the condition of man was to be a morally diseased creation."[15] When he put this into theological terms, this is how he expressed his notion of the morally diseased creation in an interview:

> Man is a fallen being. He is gripped by Original sin. His nature is sinful and his state perilous. I accept the theology and admit the triteness, but what is trite is true; and a truism can become more than a truism when it is a belief passionately held. I looked round me for some convenient form in which this thesis might be worked out and found it, in the play of children. I have lived for many years with small boys, and understand and know them with awful precision. I decided to take the literary convention of boys on an island, only make them, real boys instead of paper cutouts with no life in them, and try to show how the shape of the society they evolved would be conditioned by their diseased, their fallen nature.[16]

Since it is a simple statement about the darkness of man's heart, it would be saying nothing that has not become a religious and perhaps even psychological common place. These comments suggests the initial idea or thesis which governs the novel. It could be summarized that the book is governed by the idea that man is a fallen creature.

Viewed in anthropological terms of the Fall, *Lord of the Flies* is a sequel to *The Inheritors*. In *The Inheritors*, Golding shows that the fragmentation of man's consciousness constitutes the Fall. W.H. Auden, in one of his poems, states how the Fall has fragmented man's consciousness into four faculties—intuition, feeling, sensation and thought. Simon, Ralph, Jack and Piggy the four main characters in the novel may be said to represent the four faculties respectively. The clash among them is in its essence symbolic of the various pulls and pressures man experiences on the existential level as a result of his fragmented consciousness.

Readers are now familiar with the most important source, R.M. Ballantyne's *The Coral Island* (1858), a nineteenth-century Victorian boys' story which Golding has admitted has a 'pretty big connection.'

Carl Niemeyer writes of *The Coral Island* that "Ballantyne's shipwrecks his three boys—Jack, eighteen, Ralph, the narrator, aged fifteen, and Peterkin Gay, a comic sort of boy, aged thirteen—somewhere in the South seas on an uninhabited coral island. Jack is a natural leader, but both Ralph and Peterkin have abilities valuable for survival. The boys' life on the island is idyllic, and they are themselves without malice or wickedness.... Ballantyne's story raises the problem of evil which comes to the boys not from within themselves but from the outside world."[17]

And he continues: "Tropical nature to be sure, is kind, but the men of this non-Christian world are bad. For example, the island is visited by savage cannibals, one canoeful pursuing another, who fight a cruel and bloody battle, observed by the horrified boys and then go away. The island is again visited, this time by pirates (i.e. white men who have renounced or scorned their Christian heritage) who succeed in capturing Ralph. In due time the pirates are deservedly destroyed and in the final episode the natives undergo an unmotivated conversion to Christianity which effects a total change in their nature, just in time to rescue the boys from their clutches. Thus Ballantyne's view of man is seen to be optimistic, like his view of English boy's pride and resourcefulness which subdues tropical islands as triumphantly as England imposes empire and religion on lawless breed of men."[18]

In *The Coral Island*, Ralph, Jack and Peterkin live an active, civilized and civilizing lives. Practical difficulties are easily surmounted; and there's a total absence of guilt and bloodshed. They are all Britons—a term they use to compliment each other—all brave, obedient and honourable. The boys are clean and godly-regenerate, empire, building boys, who know by instinct how to turn paradise into a British protectorate.

The Coral Island could be used as a document in the history of ideas; it belongs to the period when boys were sent out of Arnoldian Schools certified free of Original sin. The setting is perfect with palm-trees, sandy beaches, a lagoon to swim in and plentiful ripe fruit for the re-enactment of that perennial and highly charged boyhood myth.

It was published in 1958, at the high tide of Victorian self-confidence, and is permeated with smug national complacency, synthetic missionary fervour and a kind of paralyzing condescension which could only blossom in a safe, stable, unreflecting society. The social and moral scale of things is clearly delineated. Britons come at the top of it, savages and pigs at the bottom. The boys kill pigs with the same unthinking self-assurance they employ to bully the natives into Christianity, or read them a moral lecture on the sin of cannibalism. The book ends with the burning of the false gods. Nothing is allowed to disrupt the emotional unity of the three boys, Jack, Ralph and Peterkin. There was absolutely no note of discord on that sweet Coral Island and this was as Ballantyne claims owing to they having been all tuned to the same key, namely, that of **love.**

Since Golding's explicit purpose is to stand the Ballantyne myth on its head—*Lord of the Flies* deliberately parodies the earlier book. Golding, with the findings of Frazer and Freud turned this myth inside out. Golding's version of the story added a metaphysical dimension absent from the original. This was occasioned by the moral crisis brought about by the war. He takes similar school boy characters, though they are now marooned not by a shipwreck but by a plane crash. The time is the future, in the aftermath of a nuclear war, moving their fortunes away from society. They attempt to construct their own self-sufficient social order on the island, but this founders in the face of terror, sin and evil, leading to an awareness of the end of innocence and the darkness of man's heart. The novel portrays a gradual reversion to the most primitive and bloodthirsty savagery. His story is a deeply pessimistic vision of human evil and it lies far beyond Victorian optimism or indeed conventional liberal dreams of human progress. Golding's children, are isolated on their desert island for a specific spiritual experiment.

Golding sees a world enormously altered by new knowledge. The patterns of human behaviour are generally explained by reference to psychic residue or infantile guilt. A world in which the myth of progress has failed; but the rival myth of necessary evil and universal guilt has come back without bringing God with it. So he thinks of the books of his childhood—*The Coral Island*, Well's *Outline of History* and observes that they are wrong about the world, because they thought cannibals more wicked than white men and Neanderthal man less worthy than his conqueror. These books have, in his own words, rotted to compost in his mind and in that compost the new myth put down roots. When it grows it explains the ancient situation to which our anxieties recall us: loss of innocence, the guilt and ignominy of consciousness, the need for pardon. Golding's work reflects a more general twentieth-century disillusionment, accentuated by experience of the Second World War.

Talking about its genesis in *The Coral Island*, Golding in an interview with Kermode records his reaction to Ballantyne's *The Coral Island* thus:

> What I am saying to myself is, "Don't be such a fool, you remember when you were a boy, a small boy, how you lived on that island with Ralph and Jack and Peterkin (boys in The Coral Island)...I said to myself finally. Now you are grown up, you are adult, its taken you a long time to become adult, but now you've got there you can see that people are not like that, that they would not behave like that; if they were God-fearing English gentlemen, and they went to an island like that."[19] Their savagery would not be found in the natives, instead they would be kind and uncomplicated. The devil would rise out of the intellectual complication of the three white men on the island itself.

Golding adopts the Ballantyne situation and characters for ironical purposes. The massive metaphorical structure with which the novel is governed is designed to assert something permanent and significant about human nature. *Lord of the Flies*, tells the story of a group of English school boys, between the ages of six and twelve, who survive a plane crash on an

Eden-like tropical island. The boys were apparently evacuated during a destructive atomic war and are left, with no adult control anywhere, about to build their own society on the island. They are confronted with the task of survival. The chance to create a new Paradise is clear enough, but Golding quickly indicates that the boys are products of and intrinsically parts of current human society. The island provides food, plenty of opportunity for swimming, and 'fun'. But a conflict quickly develops between the boys, led by Ralph, who would keep a fire going (they cherish some hope of rescue) and build adequate shelters and those led by Jack, originally members of a choir, who would burn wild pigs and give full reign to their predatory and savage instincts.

First the boys proceed to set up a rational society based on a 'grown-up' model. So to begin with the children impose 'civilized' standards of conduct on their small community. As Jack observes, in a recognizable parody of Ballantyne, "We've got to have rules and obey them. After all, were not savages. We're English, and the English are best at everything, so we've got to do the right things" (p. 47). In the first democratic meeting they elect a leader, Ralph. They have a meeting place for discussion and a conch-shell to summon them. This conch also becomes a symbol of rational behaviour, harmony and order. No one may speak unless he is holding it. It is the possession of the conch that more than anything else qualifies Ralph to be the chief. As Ralph, Jack and Simon explore the island, they are aware of 'a kind of glamour that was spread over them and the scene...' (p. 27). But soon this glamorous world starts breaking up. Just as the embryo in the womb recapitulates evolutionary development, so these young boys are slipping back on the path that leads to primitivism. The rational democracy is not able to cope very well with the fears of the younger boys.

Gradually, conditions being right for it, the shibboleths of twentieth-century civilization are erased with appalling ease from these middle-class boys' mind. Almost immediately the society disintegrates under two pressures—aggression and superstition. First come irrational fears of imaginary monsters;

the dark unknown which descends at night assumes a monstrous identity and is propitiated by totemic pigs head as the best. There is a feeling that there is something behind them all the time in the jungle. Their collective anger turns against a human victim. Hunting becomes killing as Jack's hunters break away from Ralph's fire-keepers to form a tribal society with gods, rituals and territory at the islands end. Not only is the conch shattered but the island itself is set on fire. Then the boys split into two groups: the hunters and those struggling to retain their civilized standards. The hunters, their initial squeamishness lost, revel in the blood-lust induced by pig-sticking. They daub their faces with coloured clay. Jack, their leader, is safe from shame or self-consciousness behind the mask of his paint. Then comes the inevitable ritual mimesis: 'Kill the pig,' they howl, dancing round its reeking, dismembered corpse, 'Cut his throat! Kill the pig! Bash him in!' (p. 82). This wild and ritualistic dance fascinate the boys. When one of the boys (Simon), having discovered the rational truth of the 'beast' at the top of the mountain (the 'beast' is a dead man in his parachute, dropped from a battle ten miles above the island), stumbles into the ritualistic dance, he is forced by Jack to enact the role of the pig. The boy is never given the time or the opportunity to make the rational truth clear, for the dancers, cloaked in frenzy and darkness kill him ritually as a totemic beast. Unable to stop others, even, to his shame, recognises some of the same dark frenzy at the centre of his own being. And Piggy, Ralph's 'brain trust' though always unattractive and unpopular, the boy whose glasses got the fire going in the first place, is killed by Jack's principal lieutenant as a political enemy. Jack is victorious. His dogmatic authority, his cruelty and his barbaric frenzy have a deeper hold on the nature of man than do Ralph's sensible regulations. "Which is better?" cries Ralph in desperation fire and rescue, or hunting and breaking things up. There is no doubt which Jack will choose. "Not the world of longing and baffled commonsense"—but the brilliant world of hunting, tactics, fierce exhilaration and skill. The forces of light and reason fail to alleviate the predatory brutality and the dark, primeval fear at the centre of man.

But the metaphor of the society the boys construct is not left to do its work alone. Just when the savage forces led by Jack are tracking down Ralph (a sacrificial victim) burning the whole island to find him in order to offer his head to the God. (Pig's head on a stick) (p. 177) a representative of the adult world in the person of a British naval officer arrives to rescue the boys. Ironically, the smoke of barbaric fury, not the smoke of conscious effort has led to rescue. Throughout the novel, frequent references to possible rescue and to the sanity of the adult world seemed the delusions of the rational innocent. Ralph and Piggy often appealed to adult sanity in their futile attempt to control their world, but, suddenly and inconsistently at the end of the novel, adult sanity really exists. The horror of the boy's experience on the island was really a childish game, though a vicious one. The British officer turns into a public school master: "I should have thought that a pack of British boys—you all British aren't you?—would have been able put up a better show than that" (p. 222). The whole statement about man at the end as Golding directly points out. Ralph has learned from the experience. 'And in the middle of them, with filthy body, matted hair, and unwiped nose, Ralph wept for the end of innocence, the darkness of man's heart, and the fall through the air of the true, wise friend called Piggy' (p. 248). But the rescue is ultimately a 'gimmick,' a trick, a means of cutting down or softening the implications built up within the structure of the boy's society on the island.

Golding created a successful adventure story about a group of boys abandoned on tropical island somewhere in the Pacific ocean. They are the victims of a war which is still raging elsewhere. Golding shows how the boys adapt to the island, learning how to make fire, to build shelters, to hunt and to maintain discipline. Initially they relish their new freedom but under the strain of their total isolation they develop tensions which finally break out into conflict. They rejected their first leader, replacing him by a boy who is better able to cope with the physical hardships of the island. The community they develop around him is aggressive but also prepared to accept his absolute authority. When rescue finally comes the boys have lost all touch with the 'civilised' values of their former existence. They have become like 'savages.' It is the civilised who are corrupt, out of phase with the natural rhythm. Their guilt is the price of evolutionary success.

The vileness proceeds not from cannibals, but from the boys. They are dirty and inefficient. They have some notion of order, symbolised by the beautiful couch which heralds formal meeting; but when uncongenial effort is required to maintain it, order disappears. The shelters are inadequate, the signal fire goes out at the very moment when Jack first succeeds in killing a pig. Intelligence fades; irrational taboos and blood-rituals make hopeless the task of the practical but partial intellect of Piggy; his glasses, the firemakers, are smashed and stolen, and in the end he himself is broken to pieces as he holds the conch. When civilized conditioning fades, Piggy's appeal to what adults might do or think becomes tedious. The children are capable of neither savage nor civil gentleness. Always a little nearer to raw humanity than adults, they slip into a condition of animality, depraved by mind, into the cruelty of hunters with their devil liturgies and torture. They make an unnecessary, evil fortress, they steal and abandon all operations aimed at restoring them to civility. Evil is the natural product of their consciousness.

The boys try to construct a civilization in the island but it breaks down in blood and terror, because the boys are suffering from the terrible disease of being human. The evil of Ballantyne's novel is wholly externalised, largely in the cannibals who live on surrounding islands. But Golding observes that one of our faults is to believe that evil is somewhere else and inherent in another nation.

The unhappy theme of the novel is 'the end of innocence' (p. 223). The loss of innocence for which Ralph weeps at the novel's close, is not a matter of transformation from childish goodness to adolescent depravity. It is not a growing into wickedness. It is rather the coming of an awareness of darkness, of the evil in man's heart that was present in the children. To acknowledge the presence of this darkness in one's heart is a necessary but devastating condition of growing up, of becoming fully and yet flawedly human.

Golding believed that the condition of man was to be a morally diseased creation; and so he traces the connection between his diseased nature and the international mess he gets himself into. He presents us with his vision of human nature and the nature of the world which we inhabit through the literary convention of the experiences of a group of children cast away on a desert island. The children are real boys instead of papercuts with no life in them. Through them he worked out his thesis as to how the shape of the society they evolved would be conditioned by their diseased, their fallen nature.

Many of the accounts of the novel place the fable in a mythic frame rather than the social or moral one, for ultimately, it derives from displaces—a familiar myth that of Earthly paradise which it handles ironically. The Christian tradition has been by far the most popular mythic framework cited by critics, though the fable itself makes no immediate or direct allusion to orthodox Christianity.

According to the workings of the myth-imagination, the source of the book is the myth of Eden, in the Book of Genesis, whereby man's first innocence is corrupted by his inability to resist sin. As Adam unparadised, the body cradle within themselves the beast of evil, 'Beelzebub' (the Hebraic original for its 'English translation' Lord of the Flies (11 Kings 1.2; the chief of the devils' in Luke 11, 15). They turn the Edenic island into a fiery hell. They begin on a note of harmony in paradisiacal surroundings, but it quickly degenerates into anarchy. The various episodes in the island are the rites-de-passage for Ralph, producing in him, 'a convulsion of the mind' (p. 84) and, initiating him into an awareness of the heart of darkness.

This myth of Original sin has appealed to writers in every generation, but Golding manages to secularize it without destroying its viability on an illustration of the human temptation to wrong. We may ask with Ralph: "...what wrong? ...what makes things break up like they do?" (p. 154). This is what the novel is about the failure to establish order. An answer is to be found, on the surface level of action "in the intellectual complications of the three main characters, in their motives and deeds, and on a deeper level, in the constitution of man's psyche in "mankinds essential illness" (p. 97).

Golding's interest in ancient Egypt and the Osiris myth has also left an indelible impression upon Golding, and its influences reverberates in the symbolism of the novel.[20] The Osirian myth interpretation illuminates man's fallen nature; and the moral lesson,[21] of Golding's novel is that we are capable of the most heinous cruelties in the service of our pride.

The 'Beastie' an important symbol appears to the reader in a variety of guises: as 'a snake-thing,' 'beast from water,' 'beast from air', and finally, as an aspect of human nature. The nature of the beast is also implied by the suggestive symbolism of the title,[22] the 'Lord of the Flies,' or Beelzebub, has been associated with the Christian devil.[23] The beastie as a snake-thing invites comparison to the serpent of the Garden of Eden.[24] In the Osiris myth the Egyptian demon Set-Typhon is represented by 'snakes'[25] and with the ascent of Christianity he was transfigured into Baal or Beelzebub.[26] Golding imputes the fallen nature of man to be related to his temptation by the subtle serpent in mythical Eden. Mankind's fallen nature is his desire to be 'wise' and 'as gods.'[27] This reduces the fallen nature of man to pride. Hence we can then attribute man ills, including war, to his vanity.

The beast's manifestation as 'from the sea,' 'from the air,' and 'in us' are all associated with war. Rescue, long awaited and desperately needed comes in the form of a trim warship off-shore, that is rescue from the sea. The dead parachutist bears a message from the adult world to the boys, from a 'battle fought at ten miles' height. This sign descends upon the boys just as their society is disintegrating, and just as Ralph cries out for a sign from the supposedly well ordered adult world, a world which, the narrator informs us, is embroiled in a cataclysmic war.[28] 'Our diseased nature, the beast in us,' leads the boys to war and barbarism just as it does in the adult world.[29]

The Osiris myth accounts for the emergence of discord and, hence, war. This demonstrates the precariousness of civilization. According to Plutarch, the demon Set-Typhon filled with envy and pride, seeks to usurp his brother's (Osiris) throne. Frustrated in his attempt to take his brother's place, Typhon tricked Osiris and drowned him. Isis, the wife of Osiris, searched for the body, regained it and concealed it in the woods. Typhon, while hunting pig during a full moon, discovered and mutilated it. A war, punctuated with "terrible deeds" and "confusion," ensued until Horus, son of Osiris, appears to have defeated Typhon. Since nature contains in itself the creation of and origin of evil as well as good, Osiris, represents good in the Universe and Typhon evil.

Typhon represents the element of soul which is passionate without reason and brutish. He personifies the overpowering, violent and proud. Typhon's desire to rule leads him to wage war against his brother. If this myth speaks to the soul of man, and man like nature contains both Osirian and Typhonic traits, then we can conclude that man is by nature proud. Man can therefore be said to be a fallen creature because of his desire to be preferred. Pride leads some to heroic exertions, but also to harm others. Thus, Typhon may be said to be heroic and sick. Pride leads to war.

Pride has various manifestations, among them honour, prestige, fame and wealth. Off-campus history, or nationalism, is but one manifestation of this deeper tragic flaw. But perhaps even more troubling for modern man, pride in our ideas has thrust our world into a mental straitjacket from which we can escape only by the most anarchic violence.[30] The virulent, global atrocities of the twentieth-century were caused by both ideological pride and nationalism. The otherwise impressive edifices are merely projections out from the self, which seeks to have its views sanctified. They are mirrors, that reflect back to us our own petty prejudices. Modern man, who can explain everything in entirely antiseptic, sanitary ways cannot, no matter how often he cleanses himself, rid himself of the decay that comes from within.

It is possible to view the boys as representatives of various instincts or elements of the personality. "The catastrophe occurs because the qualities of intelligence, address, bravery, decency, organization and insight are divided among Piggy, Jack, Ralph and Simon. Each of them lacks some vital gift; none of them is a complete person.[31] E.M. Forster declares that it is just this fragmentation that is responsible for their regression.[32] One critic argues that the fragmentation correspond to Plato's division of the human soul. Golding is careful to point out that it is Ralph's administrative duties—an image of the soul's balance and power when grounded by reason that enable him to keep the anarchy that resides in his heart under control.[33]

The Typhonic element of human nature, in the novel is represented by Jack. He is red-haired freckled, hence ruddy and prone to blush when angry and frustrated. Typhon according to the tradition is described as red and ruddy. When Jack's face "blushes with mortification, on the election of Ralph, he can be said to be red. And again after the second vote, "Jack turned, red in face" because he had been outwitted (p. 115). Jack desires to be preferred, and when his pride is offended he blushes. Jack is envious, proud and red, his blushing appears as a manifestation of wounded pride. He evinces an overweening ambition and a hunting desire to be chief, demonstrated by this competition with Ralph, both when the boys first selected a chief and when Jack calls for a vote of 'No-confidence' in Ralph. After his second preliminary defeat, Jack responds by creating his own society and waging war on Ralphs.

Ralph and Jack are vitally different in their natures, upbringing and attitudes "...two continents of experience and feeling unable to communicate" (p. 60). Their two worlds are essentially incompatible. "...the brilliant world of hunting, tactics, fierce exhilaration, skill (and) the world of longing and baffled commonsense" (p. 77). They're always at cross-purposes. The first note of antagonism is struck on the question of priority. While Ralph says, "The best thing we can do is to get ourselves rescued!" (p. 58), Jack replies, "Rescue? Yes of course! All the same I'd like to catch a pig first" (p. 58). Late in the scene of final confrontation between the two groups, Piggy tries in vain to make Jack and his savages see reason "which is better to be a pack of painted niggers like you, or to be sensible like, Ralph is? ...to have rules and agree, or to hunt and kill?" (p. 199). It is a clash of will, the rational will aiming at decent, democratic leadership based on reason, and irrational will seeking to establish an authoritarian regime. They are an image of the tragic state of world politics in the mid twentieth-century and of the seemingly eternal need of civilization to find rivals with whom to quarrel. Jack's ego reverts to savagery and the narrator describes it as 'demented' (p. 92). It is the antithesis of the society he opposes, the society made possible by Piggy and his spectacles.

Piggy's main persecutor is Jack, who from the first evinces hatred and contempt for Piggy, whom be seems to regard as an upstart. Jack's education seems to have instilled in him the belief that it is right to command, to rule, "I ought to be chief," said Jack with simple arrogance, because "I'm chapel chorister and head boy" (23). His privileged choir-school has no doubt taught him much about the necessity of hierarchies, including the notion that head boy from such a school ought to be topman anywhere. Whitley comments, 'The assumption of leadership bred by being part of civilized elite, is maintained when he becomes a member of a primitive elite. The perfect becomes the perfect savage.[34] The will to power in its irrational form, caring little for the immediate practical needs, is the guise evil assumes and the resultant havoc wreaked on the environment is well depicted.

Ted E. Boyle has remarked that Golding is "convinced that without the restraint of social order the human being will sink below the level of the beast."[35] This is exactly what happens to Jack.

Jack and his coharts are introduced in a way which is ominous. They appear to Ralph from the distance as a dark creature wending its way to the platform from where he has blown the conch. 'With the diamond haze of the beach **something dark** was fumbling along. The creature was a party of boys.... Their bodies...were hidden by **black** cloakes. The boy who controlled them was dressed **in the same way** (pp. 20-21). This suggests that evil exists as a potentiality in Jack. The 'opaque mad look' (p. 58), slamming his knife into a tree trunk and looking around challengingly, the offhand authority in his voice, and such other postures—all indicate his ungovernable energy and perpetual restlessness. He has already imposed his will upon the choir boys who follow him with abject obedience. He recalls with a sense of pride how "they closed in on the struggling pig...had outwitted a living thing, imposed their will upon it, taken away its life like a long satisfying drink" (p. 76). The infernal incantation—"Kill the pig; cut her throat! Bash her in" (p. 82)—is but a disguise, like the paint on his face, for his emotional self-indulgence. When he finally breaks away from Ralph and becomes the chief of his tribe, he shows himself susceptible to the totalitarian temptation and empowers himself with titanic evil. "Power lay in the brown swell of his forearms; authority sat on his shoulder and chattered in his ear like an ape" (p. 165).

The confrontation between the representation of order and the forces of chaos takes place when Ralph, accompanied by Piggy and the twins, Samneric, visit the castle rock, the stronghold of Jack. The twins Samneric, with all their goodness and vitality are Ralph's most loyal supporters. They are kind, loyal and generous. Their apparent blending into one another makes them representative of average everyday man. We sympathise strongly with this group and abominate Jack and Roger. Samneric are captured and forced to turn savages in the violent clash. It is as though civilization had been forced into subjugation by brute force. Piggy holds up the conch and appeals for order. But the fragile shell is nothing before the fierce anarchic tendencies of Jack and his men. Roger, Jack's henchman, let's fall a huge rock which strikes hard and drives him to his violent death with the talisman in his hands exploding into pieces. The evil of Roger is inexplicable, in part because he is a shadowy character, about whose background we know almost nothing. But Golding is determined that we should confront the Roger within us, "the reason why its no go" (p. 158). There is no escape from the agony of being human, no possibility of erecting Utopian political systems where all will go well. We have the very unpleasant feeling that we are being hunted by Jack and Roger. We fear and loathe their extravagant and insatiable evil.

Jack and his men, next, turn their attention to Ralph who runs away and conceals himself in the forest. The pig-hunt degenerates into man-hunt. The savages with their paint and spears spread terror. The whole forest is seen 'with flame' (p. 222). Ralph is horrified at his own plight. With Piggy and his conch gone, all order and sense are lost. He finds himself on outcast, alienated and isolated. In trying to come to terms with the outer world, he discovers the horrible inner self of man. Ralph weeps 'for the end of innocence, the darkness of man's heart...' (p. 223). The moment of his anguish and terror is also the moment of self-knowledge.

The protagonist Ralph is the 'average rather more than average man of goodwill and commonsense.'[36] Yet he is the man who makes mistakes because he simply does not understand at first the nature of the disease from which they all suffer. This change is exemplified by two pictures of Ralph. The first when he discovers he is on a real desert island he delights in the discovery. He feels at home with Nature, like Adam in the Garden of Eden, "He jumped down from the terrace...with excited eyes" and there is essential decency of Ralph as 'the fair boy' whose eyes proclaim 'no devil,' who tries to keep the other boy's eyes on the values of civilization. He tries to keep "a clean flag of flame flying (pp. 8, 11, 45). This is innocence and hope. He assures them "It's a good island until the grown-ups came to fetch us we'll have fun" (p. 38). The boys imagine that they can have fun not only in swimming and hunting but on imposing decent civilized English values upon their island as Robinson Crusoe had done by converting his island to an English gentleman's country estate or as Ralph, Jack and Peterkin had done on Coral Island. Ralph seems to be the civilized counterpart to Jack.

Ralph longs for a return to civilization. He is drawn to become a savage, but the idea of rescue and going home is more attractive. He would like to put on war-paint and be a savage. But, he also reminds himself that he must keep the fire burning for without the fire they can't be rescued. His instinctual relationship with the world starts fading away as he aligns himself with the rational Piggy who says, "We've got to do something" (p. 13). They convene an assembly to organize themselves in the island. It is the beginning of their efforts to establish an orderly life, but they find that the boys degenerate into a state of anarchy. The four assemblies clearly record their steady decline from harmony to chaos.

Rescue, fire and Piggy's glasses are all linked to civilization, the adult world and home. The hunters ignore the idea of rescue in favour of irrationality and savagery. To Ralph, the hunters society is "demented," their realistic belief in and appeasement of the breast seems to be the "breaking up of sanity" (p. 96). Reason becomes connected to goodness and those boys who stick by law and order, civilization and rescue; and unreasonable behaviour is linked to evil and those boys who become savages.

Both Ralph and Piggy who stand for civilization, extol the reasonable virtues of the adult world. "They wouldn't quarrel—or talk about a beast" (p. 103). But this adult-worship is misplaced because adults would quarrel. The reason, the boys are on the island is due to an adult quarrel. The difference is that the adults would rationalise the beast into an energy, either rationalistic or ideological and batter against it.

The adult world and the savages are no different from each other, except that one lies to itself, derives its unreason and claims to be civilized. Ralph represents the perspective that would conceal the true nature of man and would rationalize acts of inhumanity. Jack is honest: "We're strong we hunt! If there is a beast, we'll hunt it down! We'll close in and beat and beat!" (p. 100). Ralph is nearly killed because of his faith in the appearance of reason which is useless when contrasted to man's true nature. His rescue is not a rescue at all if it marks a return to a reflection of the society that has tried to kill him on the island. It must represent some kind of a defeat for him in view of what he at last recognizes about the nature of all men. What is traced through Ralph is a failure of reason.

Ralph is also twice confronted with just such a primal confrontation like that of Simon—Ralph before the skull of the pig and Ralph before the savage. We earlier see that he cannot connect with primal nature. For instance, standing at the island's rocky shore 'on a level with the sea' (p. 136), he follows the ceaseless, 'bulging passage' (p. 136) of the waves and feels, 'damped down,' 'helpless' and 'condemned' (p. 137) by a 'leviathan' (p. 131) monster with 'arms of surf' and 'fingers of spray' (p. 137). He cannot accept Simon's intuitive and correct faith, when the latter whispers 'you'll get back all right' (p. 137), that man can escape the 'brute obtuseness' (p. 137) of nature. After the deaths of Simon and Piggy, Ralph stands in the clearing confronted by the same offensive Head. He looks at the skull that seemed to jeer at him cynically (p. 227). Once again the darkness is depicted as resting 'about on a level with his face' (p. 228) and the skulls 'empty sockets seemed to hold his gaze masterfully and without effort' (p. 228). But unlike Simon, he turns away from acknowledging his own nature and makes a monster there 'A sick **fear and rage** swept him. Fiercely he hit out at the filthy thing in front of him that bobbed like a toy and came back, still grinning also into his face, so that he lashed and cried out in loathing' (p. 228).

Ralph cannot penetrate this 'parody thing' which in its motion amalgamates the parachutist's bowing, the 'black ball[s] (p. 180) bobbing, and the seas breathing (p. 131). All three motions are those of an ancient primal rhythm that does not 'progress' as endure a 'momentous rise and fall' (p. 137). It is the rhythm of man's darkness, 'thus minute-long fall and rise and fall' (p. 131) and man's history. It is the rhythm that transfigures Simon in death, that engulfs the parachutist on the way to sea: "on the mountain-top the parachute filled and moved; the figure slid, rose to its feet, falling, still falling, it sank towards the beach..." (p. 189) and the rhythm that imparts to Piggy some beauty. The water becomes "luminous round the rock forty feet below, where Piggy had fallen" (p. 234). Yet for Ralph, the ordinary man, "it is a terrifying rhythm," the "age-long nightmares of falling and death" (p. 235) that occur in darkness, intimating the 'horrors of death' (p. 228).

Golding indicates that once atavistically in contact with this dark rhythm, at the centre of the self, man will no longer be, in Ralph's words, 'cramped into this bit of island, always on the lookout' (p. 125). If man is prepared to face his face, he may escape (in symbolic terms) the island.

Ralph, is given just such an opportunity. In his last desperate race (depicts in the penultimate scene) Ralph hides himself in Simon's cell, 'the darkest hole' (p. 242) of the island. Like Simon he is in terror with primal nature: "He laid his check against the chocolate-coloured earth, licked his dry lips and closed his eyes" and feels "under the thicket, the earth was vibrating very slightly" (p. 234). Jerking his head from the earth, he peers into the 'dulled light' and sees a body slowly approaching waist knee, two knees, two hands, a spear sharpened at both ends.

A head, Ralph and someone called a 'savage' (p. 244) peer through the obscurity at each other repeating in their action Simon's scrutiny before the Head.

> You could tell that he saw light on this side and on that, but not in the middle—there. In the middle was a blob of dark and the savage wrinkled up his face, trying to decipher the darkness. (p. 243)

Just at the moment his eyes connect with those of the savage, Ralph repeats Simon's early important admonition "You'll get back" (p. 245) and with this partial acknowledgement of his own savagery he breaks through the cell. Expecting nothing he strikes out, screaming:

> He forgot his wounds, his hunger and thirst, and became fear; hopeless fear on flying feet, rushing through the forest towards the open beach. (p. 245)

Rushing, screaming through the fire that undulates 'forward like a tide' (p. 245) screaming and rushing and 'trying to cry for mercy' (p. 246), he trips, all falls on the ground, sees, before him, the officer. In a way he is saved; or given mercy.

His efforts towards a civilized state are a dismal failure. Things fall apart or 'break-up' in Roger's phrase (p. 89) into atavism, savagery and bloodshed. The boy's regress to a state of nature. The experience of this is not of an earthly paradise but a hell on earth.

The tropical island which seems to be the boy's paradisiacal in its unspoilt wildness proves to be an inferno, a sort of pressure cooker heated by the vertical sun which aims blows at the boys' head in its violent intensity which fires 'down invisible arrows' (p. 67) like an angry or malevolent God. The reality of nature on the tropics is profoundly sinister and threatening. From their experience of this natural environment the boys derive a sort of religion, but their theology is demonology, the Lord or God is a devil.

The interpretation that Ralph is a reasonable character is damned by his attraction to the seductions of hunting, fierce exhilaration and ambition. Eric Smith comments that Ralph "sticks by 'law and rescue,' rather than 'hunting and breaking thing up,' yet he gradually approaches the savagery of Jack and his tribe...he cannot understand why, as he plays almost a double part, they cannot accept him as harmless."[37] In the incident where Ralph almost maims Robert in the ecstasy of a pig killing ritual he was 'carried away by a sudden thick excitement' and overmastered by a desire to 'squeeze and hunt' (p. 104). More damning is his participation in yet another pig ritual: the murder of Simon. He demonstrates that he too can be carried away by mad frenzy.

Ralph at the end of the novel, on the precipice, stares uncomprehendingly into the irrational darkness of his soul. He cries for the loss of innocence and for the loss of his rational friend Piggy, who also denied the irrational. According to Baker, the boys have committed a sin, by trying to impose "in their innocent pride" an order on the "vital chaos of their nature."[38] Their attempt in the form of parliamentary government failed and they regress into barbarism. The plight of the boys becomes an allegory for the plight of modern man, who denies and fears the irrational. Mankind's essential illness is irrational fear. Fear, the dead parachutist, and various other manifestations of the beast are symbols and point to the vital core of the novel.

What we have with Ralph is not the development of a heroic insight but a study in failure. He fails when he tries to act reasonably against the hunters because he thinks that adults would act reasonably. But civilization denies the darkness of its heart. It covers it with a veneer of reason and then goes out into the world and fights wars, it acts in the same way as Jack and the hunters, except that it is far, far more destructive. Ralph tries to hide the beast in himself by a worship of the adult world. And yet, if at the end Jack and his painted tribe armed with sharpened sticks reflect the well-armed and uniformed officer and his men, Ralph's advocacy of rational behaviour has been nothing but a misplaced advocacy of an illusion or miscomprehension. He has worshipped the lie behind which man attempts to conceal his true nature. Ralph himself displays the rending of this lie when he finds himself longing to hurt Robert—"The desire to squeeze and hurt was over-mastering" (p. 126) and at the end of the novel he has become an efficient savage. Reasonable naval officer and unreasonable savage are reflection of each other. Ralph's failure is that he does not understand this until the end, and Piggy remains ignorant of it.

The linking of the forces of reason to the beast is a logical progression throughout the novel. Ralph pretends to machine-gun Piggy: "Ralph...returned as a fighter plane...and machine gunned Piggy" (p. 12). This prophetically relates Piggy to the beast. Ralph's action reflects the adult world's pursuit of enemies which also parallels the hunters' pursuit of Ralph. Pig, piggy, beast and Ralph are gradually merged during the novel. Later, Jack asks Ralph if he is "coming?" up the mountain in search of pig. this prefigures his "coming" (p. 131) when he challenges Ralph to come up the mountain in search of the beast. Pig and beast are linked, and the tribes' hunting of pig and then of Ralph relates Ralph to the beast. The civilized world has created the beast by providing a corpse which the boy can realise as the beast. The relationship between reason and the beast as inseparable is clear from the start.

If a traumatic experience was necessary for Ralph to realize the power of darkness, Simon has an intuitive grasp of it. Jack and his followers, like the new men in *The Inheritors* and the boys in *The Coral Island* externalize the Beast and placate it by animal sacrifice. But Simon, the strange visionary child, and Golding's 'saint,' encounters and recognizes the meaning of the Beast. The introspective Simon's communion with the Lord of the Flies, which may be called the key episode of the book, is but a communion with, and a recognition of, the powers of darkness within himself and within everybody. Simon's quest, is the fables major pursuit, for he is used as a mouthpiece for what Golding has called, as one of the conditions of existence.

The Lord of the Flies asserts in the voice of a school master and delivers something very much like a Sermon. It insists that the island is corrupt and all is lost. "There is not anyone to help you. Only me And I'm the Beast." Simon's mouth laboured, brought forth audible words:

> 'Pig's head on a stick.' Fancy thinking that the head was something you could hunt and kill! said the head. 'For a moment or two the forest and all the other dimly appreciated place echoed with a parody of laughter. You knew, didn't you? I'm part of you.' (p. 158)

He dismisses the talking head with a rational formula, 'pig's head on a stick,' which has been described as a courageous denial of the heads view of itself![39]

After he communes with the Lord of the flies, Simon comes across the 'beast'—'a humped thing' (p. 161)—suddenly sitting up in the strong wind and looking down at him. He discovers that it is but the dead parachutist who had been a victim in an air battle the adults were fighting ten miles above the sea, and had come drifting down, eventually setting among the rocks on the mountain. So the beast which the boys greatly feared is a human, 'harmless and horrible' (p. 162). Simon is thus able to release the parachutist, the 'beast' from the 'wind's indignity' and sets out to free the boys from the ignominy of fear. His efforts to communicate his knowledge to other prove fatal to him.

He desires to tell the boys below about 'mankind's essential illness' (p. 111). "Whenever Simon thought of the beast there arose before his inward insight the picture of a human at one heroic and sick" (p. 113). He does not need to learn anything from the beast and he does not. A series of question is posed to which he already knows the answer. "I'm part of you?... I'm the reason. Why it's no go? Why things are what they are?" (p. 158). The truth comes to Simon in the form of a revelation. (A revelation is a mysterious way of knowing that is implanted in the receiver, who as a consequence becomes a knower. It is neither a speculation nor a chain of reasoning based upon observation. Moses, for example, faithfully accepts the revelation that he will lead the Israelites from bondage in Egypt. It's not that words cannot describe the prophetic vision, but rather the veracity of its claim is unquestionable).

Like Moses with the tablet of the law, he brings the truth down from the mountain. But because of the fainting fit he has had, Jack and his savages in the extreme frenzy of tribal dance mistake him for the beast and kill him before he can communicate the healing truth or comfortable knowledge.

Simon attempts to articulate his vision of the beast with, 'the dirtiest thing there is.' Jack's crude monosyllabic response literally ruin's Simon's effort. The reader is left to wonder what the dirtiest thing is, Jack's response, and how they relate to the beast. From the vantage point of young boy we may infer that excrement, which can be conveyed in one crude syllable, is the dirtiest thing. 'Shit' is in us, entirely natural, and yet invisible like the beast. Like the beast, it too evoked revulsion when it becomes manifest. Simon's inspired image and Jack's reply are apt. Simon may not have been able to articulate his message, because by its very nature, it cannot be rationally defended. Simon would have been unable to persuade the other boy even if he could find the words. He is ridiculed.

Simon has learnt that, the beast was harmless and horrible, and the news must reach the other as soon as possible. But the frenzied hunters will not listen to him: they tear him limb from limb in a ritual orgy, while he is still shrieking about a dead man upon the hill. Man, Golding seems to be saying, cherishes his guilt, his fears, his taboos and will crucify any saint or redeemer who offers to relieve him of his burden by telling the simple truth. There is a horrible symbolic appropriateness about the corpse itself: the nameless devil and its victims are identical. Evil is ineradicable: the Earthly Paradise is a delusion. Man's heart is dark, and no innocence lives beneath the sun, or if it does, it must, inevitably suffer and die as Piggy and Simon died; their wisdom and virtue destroyed by the Beast's devotees. It is their defence against an imagined external Beast which allows the beast within them to gain absolute control and to transform them into murderers.

Simon's recognition of evil and all mankind's complicity occasions his ritual death. He meets the fate of those who remind society of its guilt. Man prefers to destroy the objectification of his fear, rather than recognize the dark terrors and evil of himself.

The name 'Simon' in Hebrew means 'the one who listens' and we can claim that the head's voice and Simon's are one and the same.[40] Whitley argues that Lord of the flies could be rendered in English us "Lord of dung" (p. 43).

But this Lord of the Dung is Simon, the Head that counsels acceptance of evil is his own strategic consciousness. Evil exists but not as a beast. The Head answers him: "We are going to have fun on this island" (p. 178), even though 'everything' is 'a bad business'. Such counselling of acceptance of evil is 'the infinite cynicism of adult life' (p. 70), the cynicism of the conscious mind.

To interpret incorrectly the Head as an objective symbol for evil, independent of consciousness, would be to make the same mistake as Jack of externalising and objectifying one's own evil. The identity of the two is worked out very carefully. The Lords' head has 'half-shut eyes' (p. 170) and Simon keeps 'his eyes shut, then sheltered them with his hand' (p. 171) so that his vision is partial. He sees things 'without definition and illusively' (p. 171) behind a 'luminous veil'. Simon feels his own savagery, he 'likes his dry lips' and feels the 'weight of his hair.' Later after his epileptic fit, the blood 'dries around his mouth and chin' (p. 180) in the manner of the 'blood-blackened' (p. 170) grinning mouth of the Head. The flies, now that the butterflies have dismissed them, detect the identity, leave the gulls and 'alight by Simon's runnels of sweat' (p. 171) and drink at his head. The Head grins at this ingenuity. By a profound effort of will, Simon forces himself to penetrate his own loathing and break through his own consciousness: 'At last Simon gave up and looked back; saw the white teeth and dim eyes, the blood and his gaze was held by that ancient, inescapable recognition' (p. 171).

It is himself he is looking at. His face (i.e. the Head) grins at the flies of corruption and he acknowledges it as himself. He prepares to penetrate mysteries and 'go down and through in darkness.' He looks into the vast mouth of hell and thereby submits to the terror of his own evil. "Simon found he was looking into a vast mouth. There was blackness within, a blackness that spread.... He fell down and lost consciousness" (p. 178). He penetrates here his own evil. Returning from non-being, he awakens next to the dark earth close by his cheek" (p. 179) and knows that he must 'do something.' He approaches the beast on the hill to discover that 'this parody,' ringed as well by green flies, is nothing more than 'harmless and horrible' than the Head. Both are man as he is. In releasing the figure 'from the rocks and...the wind's indignity (p. 181) he frees himself.

If the beast is in man, reason and unreason belong together. Man tends to regard himself in moral terms; the reasonable man can rationalize unreasonable and inhuman behaviour against other men by regarding him as an enemy. The death of Simon is, therefore, a condemnation of Ralph who supported rational and civilized values on the island. Simon's powerlessness when possessed of this knowledge shows that all man are at the mercy of their nature, which is basically the same whether applied to Piggy, the officer or the savages.

Golding refers to Simon as a "Christ-figure."[41] He reminds one of Christ and other martyrs who initially are not understood by their fellowmen and meet with the inevitable tragic end. The tragedy of Simon may be regarded as yet another triumph of evil forces and a setback to man's quest for truth, beauty and goodness.

The truth which Simon offers is a grim one, but Simon is not at all a grim or a dark figure. He is affectionate, gentle and kind, helping the littluns to find good fruit, for example, but he is also a loner, a 'queer' boy who isolates himself in a forest glade reminiscent of a church and goes into reveries. The other boys regard this youthful mystic as mad or a fool.

The traditional role of the prophet is to awaken men to the truth of their sinfulness. Simon does this and he also succeeds in fulfilling the popular view of the prophets task by foretelling the future. He tells Ralph that he will get home safely and his voice comes to Ralph just before he is rescued. The boys live in the terror of believing that the Beast is an evil creature at the mountain-top, so Simon the prophet goes to the mountain to discover the truth. On his way he finds a forest glade desecrated by a Sow's head on a stick, a gift for the Beast. Simon falls into a fit or hallucination, or vision, in which the Lord of the flies, the Devil, speaks to him through the foul mouth of the head and tells him that he is 'part of you.' He warns Simon to go back or the boy will 'do' him (pp. 157-59). Simon, defies the threat, climbs the mountain finds the parachutist and descends to the beach to be slaughtered.

Amidst the bloody chaos of the storm and the demonic dance, we are told that 'Simon was crying out something about a dead man on a hill (p. 168) as he is being assaulted. He refers to the parachutist, but we also hear a suggestion of the death of Christ on Calvary and realise, that in killing the true prophet who had come down to reveal to them their real nature, their sinfulness and thus set them on the road towards saving themselves, the boys are re-enacting the crucifixion of Christ. Simon's life and death are the initiation of Christ. In ascending the mountain and returning to the boys, despite the warnings of the Lord of the flies about what will happen to him, he takes up and shares the cross like his namesake from Cyrene Simon. "He helps," as Ralph earlier remarks (p. 59). His self-sacrifice does not, however, achieve an instant conversion of the boys. Nor did Christ's with regard to mankind as a whole.

Piggy blames him for bringing his death on himself: "coming in the dark—he had no business crawling like that out of the dark. He was batty. He asked for it" (p. 173). He walked right into his own death, so he must have been mad, a fool, a simple Simon.

Simon initiates the folly of that Supreme Christ, who allowed himself to be crucified and whose teaching must seem foolish to the worldly-wise. Christ the holy fool is admirably described by Erasmus in the *Praise of Folly*: Christ too, though he has the wisdom of the father, was made something of a fool himself in order to help the folly of mankind, when he assumed the nature of man and was seen in man's form. Nor did he wish them to be redeemed in any other way save by the folly of the cross and through his simple, ignorant apostles to whom he unfailingly preached folly.[42]

To those in darkness or to those under the sway of the Lord of this world, who is the Lord of the flies, the wisdom of Christ must appear utter folly. Simon is the first of Golding's holy fools, characters who in many respects are holy or Christ-like and yet for the same reason, ill-fitted for survival in the world of fallen man.

The knowledge which Simon offers—that the beast is within us, that we acknowledge the 'thing of darkness' as our own is disturbing and negative. He does not appear to bring the good news of redemption or salvation. But his life and death offer some hope in the book's pervasive gloom, that among all the boys, atleast one good man has been found—one person who is capable of initiating Christ's redemptive example. At the mountain top he is able to free the dead pilot, according to Golding a symbol of the nightmare of human history, just as Christ changed the nature of history by freeing man from the bondage of sin, offering the possibility of escape from the endless backsliding and tribulations of human and personal history. We are given an 'eloquent and transfiguring' description of the seas disposal of Simon's body. Simon is carried towards the open sea by the tide, attended by 'strange moonbeam-bodied creatures with fiery eyes' who weave a halo of brightness around his head (pp. 169-70). It is Simon's self-sacrifice that transforms these creatures to beauty, redeeming the world of nature and re-establishing its beauty and harmony.

Golding's depiction of Simon as a 'Saint' carries definite Christian connotation. But a saint is, as Chesterton revealed, "a medicine because he is an antidote. Indeed that is why the saint is often a martyr; he is mistaken for a poison because he is an antidote."[43] Simon represents the antidote for rationalism that cannot see. Simon's insight into the beast offers the boys the possibility of salvation on the island, not as we know in heaven. Simon's knowledge, had it been believed, would have made up for the defects in Piggy. Piggy's knowledge coupled with the ability to see beyond mere appearance would have made Ralph's regime resilient to the inroads of Jack's barbarism.

Simon and Piggy represent two warnings ways of looking at the world, which occur frequently in Golding's fiction. Faith in science and rationality, with a marked disbelief in anything supernatural is characteristic of Piggy. Simon by contrast is intuitive, introspective, other worldly; his central insight is gained in a vision or trance. Simon represents and has access to a dimension of experience which is religious.

The character of Piggy is firmly grounded in reality by his nickname, one common in English schools and one which immediately conjures up a physical appearance: fat, clumsy, generally good natured and not very good at games. From this naturally follows the extension into excessive rationality, yoked with physical discomforts as myopia, asthma, diarrhoea and sweat. He has a lower-class tone and ungrammatical diction. He is the voice of reason. At every turn Piggy fulfils the requirements of realism. Although Ralph discovers the conch, Piggy knows what it is and how to use it. Most important of all, Piggy sees the need for a meeting. Once the boys are gathered, Piggy "moved among the crowd asking names and frowning to remember them" (p. 17). Not Ralph, but Piggy knows the importance of assemblies, Piggy can, for these reasons be deemed the true founder of the parliamentarian society, created by the assembly. At the start of the novel, the narrator states "what intelligence had been shown was traceable to Piggy" (p. 21).

From the moment we first see the boy on the island, Piggy appears as a Knower. He has an inkling of chaos into which the adult world has fallen. He understands that their coming to be on the island is linked to the war raging outside. He attempts to dispel the irrational fear of the littluns by rational account of fear and the beast. Speaking of 'doctors...for the inside of your mind,' Piggy concludes that fear is in the beholder; it does not result from a healthy apprehension of the unknown.

Piggy rightly condemns the notion that there is an external beast that lives in the forest or the sea, but under great pressure comes to believe that Jack is the Beast or the Devil, failing to see that this too is an externalisation, an avoidance of his own guilt. Piggy's scientific views dictate that there is no Devil in the world, but if he must allow that there is evil, he is determined to 'believe that evil is somewhere else' and in someone else. Above all he rejects Simon's suggestion that the beast is a reality within themselves.

He questions whether the island can sustain a beast. He asks, "what would a beast eat?" (p. 75). The obvious and ironic answer with derision is that it would eat pig. He goes on to precipitate the debate that makes the boys' undoing by asking Phil to recount his experience of the beast. Phil's tortured rambling initiates a chain of events that would lead the narrator to relate, 'that the world, that understandable and lawful world was slipping away (p. 82). Had Piggy been an acute observer of men or boys, he would have realised how fragile the island society had become and foreseen the impact of Phil's tale.

Piggy's lack of prudence points to another fatal blow in his understanding. He proves incapable of diagnosing the disease that afflicts the boy, he cannot see the beast for what it is, and he refuses to admit that Simon's death was murder. Calling it an accident, he refuses even to acknowledge his participation. He rationalizes the entire incident by arguing, 'He hadn't no business crawling like that out of the dark. He was batty. He asked for it (p. 143). Piggy denies the moral implication of their collective guilt. He coldly declares, "We never done nothing, we never see nothing, Piggy's reason ill-equips him to understand the nature and origin of evil. Piggy's scientific humanism precludes him from seeing the beast in us. The author has Piggy proclaim the credo of scientific humanism. "Life is scientific that's what it is" (p. 76).

Scientific humanism, which is faith in the progressive and liberating power of science and man's ability to rationally posit values, has stripped man of the religious context which gave his life meaning. Confidence in mankind's ability to conquer nature and prejudice gave modern man the sensation that undreamed of possibilities were now open to him. However, recent history and they myriad of variation on the philosophy of Friedrich

Nietzsche indicate that scientific humanism precludes us from positing any value; that is, it precludes us from seeing evil for what it is. The scientific humanist, the 'model intellectual,' is 'literally in a state of free fall,'[44] into the abyss of nihilism.

Baker regards Piggy in what he takes as a Promethean aspect[45] and argues Piggy's empirical disavowal of the 'beastie'—'Life...is scientific, that's what it is.' In a year or two when the war's over they'll be travelling to Mars and back. I know there's no beast...' (p. 105) is an evidence of intellectual hubris which must be punished. Greek myth is invoked. The final punishment of those who denied the god of nature is to render them conscious of their awful crimes and to cast them out from their homeland as guilt-stricken exiles and wanderers upon the earth.

The limitation of Piggy's practical intelligence are highlighted by comparison with Simon. Piggy's clever and sensible schema fail to bring about the rescues the boys' desperately need: his rational approach is unable to sway the mass of boy's in debate or preserve order among them.

Piggy's lone voice of reason is unheeded, as man succumbs to the violence and irrationality within. Piggy's knowledge is rooted in modern science and deduction from empirical observation. Only that which can be demonstrated in the light of day is real and rational. Piggy lacks practical wisdom; he doesn't understand people.

Jack's hatred and violence towards Piggy is the raw naked truth about England's social organization. Classist attitudes not only ensure that under the motto of fair play a very unfair deal is given to most members of the society, they also bring about the reification of people. A person is treated not on the merits of his complex make-up as an individual but merely in accordance with him being recognized as a component of a mass class-group. From the very outset, Piggy is isolated stranded on an island within the island, by being lower-class. Even Ralph, a good natured boy, seems reluctant initially to accept the friendship of the one companion he has so far found on the desert island.

What's you name?

"Ralph"

The fat boy wanted to be asked his name in turn but this proffer of acquaintance was not made.... "One has the feeling throughout this scene that Ralph has been conditioned to be unfriendly towards boy who talk like Piggy. Ralph is not slow to inform Piggy that his father is officer class, but in response to the crucial question. "What's your father?" Piggy can produce only the poignant reply: "My dad's dead," he said quickly "and my mum—" (p. 14). The unseemly haste with which Piggy announces that his father is dead suggests a reluctance to reveal his place in life and the blank after the mention of his Mum speaks unhappy volumes. "Piggy has failed to produce satisfactory credentials. It is partly for this reason that Piggy is doomed to become the centre of social derision so that everyone felt cheerful and normal" (p. 164).

The final blow dealt to Piggy transforms the extraordinary and miraculous complexity and beauty of his brain, the seat of consciousness and what makes the unique person he is into mere "stuff." For all his practical sense, he is quite unable to do away with the violent passions and anarchic emotions which drive him to his terrible doom.

Piggy's tragic end occurs at the Head. It is the slaughter of a pig for he is decapitated by "a glancing blow from chin to knees" (p. 222). Travelling through the air, with a grunt he lands on the square red rock in the sea, a sacrificial table. And the monster-sea sucks his body, which "like a pig after it has been killed, twitched" (p. 223). His head is smashed, the stuff comes out and turns red, and Ralph, running along the rocky neck, jumps just in time to avoid the "headless body of (sacrificial) sow" (p. 223). His death underlines the inadequacy of the rational mind as a total human response to life.

The symbol of the severed Head of the pig, where Piggy meets his death and to which Simon turns in distaste and awe and from which he tries to escape at first is at the heart of the fable's mythopoeia. Grinning cynically its mouth gaping and its eyes half-closed, the Head is placed on a rock in a sea-like clearing before Simon's cabin-island. It is a symbol which operates macrocosmically as well as microcosmically. The castle rock at the islands end is like a severed head too—it mirrors the pig's head. "Soon in a matter of centuries" (p. 130) this Head will be severed. At the story's conclusion giggling black and green savages swarm around and over it the black and green flies swarm around the Lord's head.

This symbolism suggests that the Head, the centre of reason—is destroyed with the death of Piggy, and as the island society regresses, the 'bridge' (p. 134) between rationality and irrationality is cut. The severed head of the soul is a symbol of corrupt and corrupting consciousness. It is a symbol for the malaise of the human consciousness which objectifies evil rather than recognise its subjectivity; this kind of moral distancing the officer commits. This intellectual complication is 'mankind's essential illness' which Simon discovers in the severed Head; it prospers on the island's Heads, Castle Rock. The English error is to objectify and externalise the Devil, as the boys do and this self-congratulatory attitude is dangerous because it allows the devil to go to work, and evils to be penetrated under the cover of the belief that the English are good, decent and fair-minded. To adopt such an attitude is to blind oneself of the evils which exist in English life. Golding exposes the truth about this evil by translating it from England to a desert island.

Simon learns to understand man's potential for evil, as Ralph does when he tries to destroy the grinning skull at the beginning of the hunt, but only succeeded in increasing his awareness of the potential for evil; Neither Ralph nor Simon could escape from it, because it was part of them.

The devil at work within all of them, demands death. The first to die is the boy with the mulberry coloured birthmark who perished in the fire on the mountain. With him others may have perished, but as in war, no one knows. They symbolise the unknown victims whose graves are unmarked. The second death is that of the fighter pilot. He is a symbol of the adult world of war, death and destruction, the world which is a mirror image of the boys world on the island. The third death is of the sow and Simon's ritualistic killing is the fourth.

Leo Strauss observed, "The very life of western civilization is the life between two codes (the biblical and Greek philosophic), a fundamental tension."[46] The separation of rational and revelatory knowledge, from Golding's perspective, "is both the essence and illness of the West. It has begotten that grain we call civilization as Frankenstein created his monster."[47] Until Simon and Piggy come together, Western civilization cannot diagnose and cure its essential illness.

The treatment meted out to Piggy makes the view that the boy's story is one of simple regression and degeneration. But such a view is completely undermined by the adventurous arrival of the naval officer at the close. He arrives to find the island paradise, lost and burning. The officer is a warrior, a killer and he is right to regard the boy's war as mere "Fun and games," because compared to the massive death-dealing of the nuclear war in which he is involved, this is very small-scale indeed. But the officer is dismayed that a group of British boys should have failed 'to put up a better show than that' (p. 248).

Show, the keeping up of a good appearance is what this ultra-English Officer is all about. The white uniform, the gold buttons, the 'trim cruiser' of the closing sentence are all signs of the officers' belief in orderliness, cleanliness and of his and his nation's belief in their moral rectitude. The officer's first kindly thought about Ralph is that he 'needed a bath, a hair cut, a nose-wipe and a good deal of ointment (pp. 221-23). But the officer is no saviour. He is doubly guilty of being a warrior on behalf of one of the world's two tribes and of sanitising the killing, the vast butchery; involved in such conflicts of cleaning and dressing it up so that it seems sane and sensible. He is able to masquerade as a peacemaker, a bringer of light to the savages. He dislikes the blood and filth of the boys. He is embarrassed by Ralph's open display of emotion, but the blood and filth are the true symbols of war or warriors and Ralph's grief is an absolutely human and appropriate reaction to the revelations of the island.

Coming from his warship, he is like a *deus ex machina* descending from the 'above' of the adult world to set things right and rescue the erring children. Despite the sinister associations of the naval officer, we hope to see him as the caring and competent God who finally intervenes man's world to stop the course of the bloody history of fallen man and restore peace forever. But there is evidence in the novel which counts against it. There seems to be no haven for the boys to be rescued to, we are told that Roger's arm was conditioned by a civilization that knew nothing of him and was in ruins (p. 67). Terrified by the Beast, Ralph complains that the 'thing squats by the fire as though it did not want to be rescued' (p. 138) and the corpse is a sign that the civilization which might rescue them has been destroyed by war.

Golding says that this dead man 'is' History.[48] All that we can give our children in their trouble is this monstrous dead adult, who's 'dead, but won't lie down'; an ugly emblem of war and decay that broods over the paradise and provides the only objective equivalent for the beast the boys imagine.

The naval officer has played a part in that war and therefore there is no comfort in seeing him as an image of God, because the image is of a flawed and irresponsible God. Instead he presents himself, 'as a human at once heroic and sick.' What desperate hope the book offers is simply the example of Simon, the acknowledgement of the 'guilt,' of the 'thing of darkness' within us, and the overcoming of guilt and darkness in generous self-sacrifice for the sake of others.

The consistent presentation of boys on a realistic level allied to a symbolic structure inverts their actions with the larger meaning, involving that capacity for evil inherent in every human heart.

The ideographic structure makes it clear that the children's experiment on the island has its constant counterpart in the world outside. Both the occasion of the boys landing on the island and the parachutist remind us that "the majesty of adult life" is another childish delusion.

The ideographic structure consists in two movements; in the first, the story is seen from the point of view of the childish protagonist, Ralph, as he gradually grows more and more aware of the island's disintegration. In the second movement, we see events from a new point of view, that of the adult officer, who is completely unaware and largely indifferent to the suffering. The coda, in conjunction with such symbols as the parachutist, indicates that adulthood is also inadequate to prevent destruction. The dead parachutist shows man's inhumanity to man; he is a legacy of barbarism in both ancient and contemporary civilization, who, Golding says, represents history; Golding writes that "what the grown-ups send them is a sign...that arbitrary sign stands for off-campus history, the thing which threatens every child everywhere, the history of blood and intolerance, of ignorance and prejudice, the thing which is dead and won't lie down..."[49] thus he haunts the boys, a haunting appropriately represented by his uncanny position and motion: "the figure sat on the mountain top and bowed and sank and bowed again" (p. 119).

The children reveal the same nature as the grown-ups whom some invoke and try to emulate. In fact the child's world on the island is a painful microcosm of the adult world, for the ruin they bring upon themselves is Universal—recall that it is atomic warfare in the air that brings about their initial descent to the island. The officer's dismal failure to comprehend the "semi-circle of little boys, their bodies streaked with coloured clay, sharp sticks in their hands" (p. 246) is itself testimony to "the infinite cynicism of adult life" (p. 170) and silent witness to the Lord of the Dung's general sway.

Throughout the narrative's first movement the children appear to have been adults dealing with adult problems. Later they become whining little boys held in control by the presence of an adult. Yet the reader cannot forget the cruelty of what has gone before. For the conch of order has been smashed; the spectacles of reason and rescue have been used to destroy the island. A tribal society has hunted down and killed two individuals. We cannot forget that Ralph's piteous weeping at the end transcends the smug cynicism of the rescue, for Ralph knows the real nature of the 'pack of British boys' (p. 248).

Ralph is saved only because the adult world intervenes, yet his rescuer is on the point of returning to 'adult' war, a nuclear war which is infinitely more extravagant in its potential disorder. Given the barbaric chaos the boys have been reduced to, the officer appears to them as order. On reflection, the reader remembers that the officer is involved in a nuclear war and is still 'order'. As the narrative progresses the reader is lulled into the belief that the adults may save the situation, yet, one detects certain ironic clues. Take the reiteration of motifs—for example the phrase—'Lets have fun' that Ralph as liberal leader introduces and which later the Head obscenely throws back at Simon—these force one to reconsider what earlier seems innocuous. The heaving of logs by Sameneric, the rolling of larger and larger stones, the several gifts to the sea, the several pig hunts, the two desperate races by Ralph—these sequences of repeated actions, placed at intervals during the story, intensify the ambiguous threat and give the illusion of speeded-up denouement. The cumulative effect on the reader is to create a sense of doom which cannot be adequately located in the narrative until its confirmation in the coda.

This brings up Golding's own explication of the thematic content of his novel. "The whole book is symbolic in nature except the rescue in the end where adult life appears, dignified and capable, but in reality enmeshed in the same as the symbolic life of the children on the island. The officer having interrupted a man-hunt, prepares to take the children off the island in a cruiser which will presently be hunting its enemy in the same implacable way. And who will rescue the adult and his cruiser."[50]

The whole thesis of the novel is miniatured in this passage from Chapter 4 of the novel.

The subsoil beneath the palm trees was a raised beach; and the generation of palms had worked loose in this the stones that had lain on the sands of another shore. Roger stooped, picked up a stone, aimed, and threw it at Henry—threw it to miss. The stone, that token of preposterous time, bounced five yards to Henry's right and fell in the water. Roger gathered a handful of stones and began to throw them. Yet there was space round Henry, perhaps six yards in diameter, unto which he dare not throw. Here invisible, yet strong, was the taboo of the old life. Round the squatting child was the prediction of parents and school and policemen and the law. Roger's arm was conditioned by a civilization that knew nothing of him and was in ruins.

We have the primeval setting ('generations of palms') and a sense of a constantly evolving nature ('stones that land on the sands of another shore) within these the novelist shows us how human society has developed a corresponding pattern of behaviour. Roger starts by throwing stones at Henry for something to do; but we perceive a struggle in his subconscious between a desire to hit Henry—it is no fun deliberately to miss a target—and the knowledge, which society has instilled in him, that it is wrong to cause hurt. The episode sums up the conflict between the moral sense of man and his inclination to do as he pleases. Golding freely uses terms like 'taboo,' 'protection' and 'civilization,' thus underlying his intentions to say something generally true about human nature in the form of a story.

It is foolish to suppose that the novel ends happily. It is a deliberate device by which to throw the story into focus. With the appearance of the naval officer, the blood thirsty hunters are instantly reduced to a group of painted urchins, led by "a little boy who wore the remains of an extraordinary black cap." Yet the reduction cannot expunge the knowledge of what they have done and what they meant to do. The abrupt return to childhood, to insignificance, underscores the argument of the narrative: that evil is inherent in the human mind itself, whatever innocence may cloak it, ready to put forth its strength as soon as the occasion is propitious. This is Golding's theme and it takes on a frightful force by being presented in juvenile terms, in a setting that a deliberately likened to the sunny Coral Island of R.M. Ballantyne.

In the escape from civilization Golding's boys have the worst of both worlds. We do not find a pastoral evocation of life on the tropical island. Their returns to a state of nature, has a very unpleasant effect on them. The littluns in particular quickly become "filthily dirty" and are affected by a "sort of chronic diarrhoea" (p. 64). Prettiness and cosiness are important element in Ralph's memories of natural wildness back in England which is limited and naïvely comfortable: The remembered cottage on the moors is out of reach and unreal, a filmy dream. One of Ralph's problem as the chief is that the boys fail to abide by the rule that only one clutch of tide-washed rocks should be used as lavatory.

Man seems to be a natural producer of filth as well as evil and one is the symbol of the other. We produce wickedness and vileness which sour our lives. Of this aspect of the boys plight Leighton Hudson writes, "The odour of decay pervade life from the diarrhoea of the littluns to Jack hunting the pigs by following their steaming dropping; the association of the Beast, the evil excrement and blood is both overpowering and purposeful."[51]

The boys from a civilized society do not seem to have learnt from civilization. They cannot exploit nature, only wreck it. Nature cannot teach them anything in the Rousseauistic or Wordsworthian traditions.

Their physical degeneration is matched by an upsurge of cruelty, bloodlust and violent rapacity as the beast, which they take to be a spirit or monster outside of themselves. It rises up within them and takes over their lives. Overwhelmed by the horrors that have entered their lives, littluns isolate themselves to wail, gibber and howl at the misery of their condition.

The peacefulness, cleanliness and reasonableness of lives makes the society an ideal towards which we humans might wish to aspire. But we are a disgusting race of passionate, violent, irrational, greedy and lustful creatures. The boys wallow in filth symbolising their propensity towards evil and their dark, perverse, psychological forces which make them incapable of behaving reasonably or organizing or maintaining order.

The overall picture of man's nature which emerges from the novel is that a return to the state of nature, an escape into primitivism, leads only to the unleashing of brutality, greed for power, sadism in the most naked and brutal forms, to the horror of orgiastic and murderous midnight dances and human heads stuck on poles. It is a grim view of human condition. There is no rescue, no way out and the ending of the novel is anything but happy. But to regard it as such would be to ignore the prophetic vision of Simon.

Golding has remarked, "I am by nature an optimist, but a defective logic or a logic which I sometimes hope desperately is defective—makes a pessimist of me."[52] The tension between optimism and pessimism, between hope, and despair is characteristic of Golding's fiction.

When questioned about the full meaning and wider implication of the book, Golding remarked: "I think the book was a kind of escape out of a drab England into the South seas—followed by a sad realization that, even if you make your surrounding beautiful, you will take yourself with you, ...I felt a tremendous visional force behind the whole book. At the end, for example, there's a scene where Ralph is fleeing from the fire on the island and the point is not just that the boy is being hunted down, but that the whole natural world is being destroyed. That idea was almost as important to me as Ralph himself: the picture of destruction was an atomic one, the island had expanded to be the whole great globe. The book concerned what human beings were doing to each other and to the world in which they lived."[53]

The boys return to nature then, is not an idyll, but a nightmare. Piggy's view of the matter, if only they would spot them, they would be saved, is a comforting view of the book, since it seems to endorse the view that our civilization is rational and peaceful. But to take such a view is to deny the beast in us. Piggy's faith in grown-ups seems to be sadly misplaced. Displaying typical commonsense and faith in the known laws of science he tries to reassure Ralph: "The trouble is...that it wouldn't work" (p. 101).

We aspire to reasonableness and would like to construct and live in rational societies, but the horrible truth is that man's organized civilization and sophisticated systems of communications have failed to work, have been destroyed or have broken down in the nightmare of nuclear war. The nature of the beast within us, the innate propensity towards violence, cruelty and selfish and self-destructive wickedness makes such optimistic schemes incapable of realization. It's heart breaking to see how friendship and fair-play are replaced by hostility and tyranny. Our civilizations are condemned as barbaric and monstrously destructive.

NOTES

1. Lionel Trilling, "Lord of the Flies," *Mid-Century* (Oct. 1962), p. 11.
2. Jack I. Biles, *Talk: Conversations with William Golding* (New York: Harcourt, 1970), p. 15.
3. Oldsey and Weintraub, *The Art of William Golding* (New York: Harcourt Brace and World, 1965), p. 16.
4. William Golding, "Fable," in *The Hot Gates*, p. 98.
5. Howard S. Babb, *The Novels of William Golding*, Second edition (New York: Colma University Press), 1986.

   Virginia Tiger, *William Golding: The Dark Fields of Discovery* (London: Calder & Boyars, 1974). Points out Simon as a "Christ-figure and a 'saint'."

   Golding's interview to Frank Kermode, "The Meaning of it all," *Books and Bookmen*, 5 (October 1959), pp. 9-10.
6. William Golding and James R. Baker, "An Interview with William Golding", *Twentieth-century Literature*, 28 (1982), pp. 165-66.

   Bernard F. Dick, *William Golding* (New York: Twayne, 1967), pp. 26-33.
7. E.L. Epstein, *Notes on Lord of the Flies*, In William Golding, *Lord of the Flies* (New York: Capricorn Books, 1959), p. 190.
8. C.B. Cox, "Lord of the Flies," *Critical Quarterly*, 2 (Summer 1960), p. 112.
9. V.S. Pritchett, "Secret Parables," *New Statesman* (August 2, 1958), p. 146.
10. William Golding, *The Hot Gates*, p. 88.
11. Frederick Karl, "The Novel as Moral Allegory: The Fiction of William Golding," *A Readers Guide to the Contemporary English Novel* (New York: Noonday Press, 1962), pp. 244-61.
12. George C. Herndl, "Golding and Salinger: A Clear Choice," *Wiseman Review*, No. 502 (Winter) (1964-65), p. 310.
13. William Golding, *The Hot Gates*, p. 86.

14. Quoted by James C. Livingston, "Commentary on William Golding's *The Spire*," *Religious Dimensions in Literature Generalised*, 'Lee A. Belford (New York: The Seabury Press, 1967), p. 7.
15. William Golding, *The Hot Gates*, p. 87.
16. *Ibid*., p. 88.
17. Carl Niemeyer, "The Coral Island Revisited," *College English*, 22 (January 1961), pp. 241-45 discusses in length Golding's use of Ballantyne's novel.
18. *Ibid*., p. 242.
19. As quoted in *William Golding* by Samuel Hynes (New York: Columbia University Press, 1964), pp. 7-8.
20. William Golding, "An Egyptian Journal" (Boston: Faber and Faber, 1985), pp. 10-12, 161-62—Golding makes it clear that he is fond of Plutarch's account of the Osiri's myth, also in "Egypt from my Inside," in *Hot Gates*, pp. 71-73 shows his interest in things Egyptian.
21. William Golding, *The Hot Gates*, p. 88.
22. John Whitley, Golding's *Lord of the Flies* (London: Edward Arnold, 1970), p. 98, p. 48.
23. Samuel Hynes, "William Golding's *Lord of the Flies*," in *Critical Essays on Golding*, ed. James R. Baker (Boston: G.K. Hall, 1988), and Epstein, p. 187.
24. Stephen Metcalf, *William Golding* (Harlow, Essex: Longman, 1975), pp. 11-12.
25. John Gywnn Griffiths, "Commentary," in *De Isis et Osiris* by Plutarch (Cambridge: University of Wales Press, 1970), p. 388.
26. Epstein, *Notes on Lord of the Flies*, pp. 418-19.
27. Genesis, 3.3-7.
28. "The Meaning of it All", *Books & Bookmen* (October 1959), pp. 9-10.
29. William Golding, *The Hot Gates*, pp. 87-88.
30. *Belief and Creativity*, p. 187.
31. Philip Drew, "Second Reading," *Cambridge Review* (Oct. 27, 1956), p. 78.
32. E.M. Forster, "Introduction to William Golding's *Lord of the Flies*" (New York: Coward McCann, 1962), pp. IX-XII.

33. Robert J. White, "Butterfly & Beast in 'Lord of the Flies," *Modern Fiction Studies*, 10 (Summer 1946), p. 165 also Baker's Article Why it is No Go: A Study of William Golding's 'Lord of the Flies' *Arizona Quarterly*, 19 (Winter 1963, pp. 293-305)—(full account of Baachae source and its relation in particular to Simon's death) traces influences of Greek literature.
34. Whitley, p. 25.
35. Ted E. Boyle, "Golding's Existential Vision," *William Golding: Some Critical Considerations*, p. 24.
36. William Golding, *The Hot Gates*, p. 89.
37. Eric Smith, *Some Versions of the Fall* (London: Croom Helm, University of Pittsburgh Press, 1973), p. 173.
38. James R. Baker, "Why its No Go," in *Critical Essays on William Golding* (New York: St. Martins Press, 1965), p. 25.
39. Peter Faulkner, *Humanism in the English Novel* (London: Elek Pemberton, 1976), p. 171.
40. Henri Talon, *Evil in the Works of William Golding* (Paris: Letters Modernes, 1966), p. 25.
41. William Golding, *The Hot Gates*, p. 97.
42. Erasmus, *Praise of Folly*, pp. 198-99.
43. G.K. Chesterton, *St. Thomas Aquinas: The Dumb Ox* (New York: Doubleday, 1956), p. 23.
44. Jack I. Biles, *Talk: Conversations with William Golding* (New York: Harcourt, 1970), pp. 79-80.
45. James R. Baker, *William Golding: A Critical Study* (New York: St. Martin's, 1965), p. 8.
46. Leo Straus, "The Mutual Influence of Philosophy and Theology," *The Independent Journal of Philosophy*, 3 (1979), p. 111.
47. "Belief and Creativity," pp. 186-87 and also in James R. Baker. "Three Decade of Criticism in critical essays on William Golding," p. 2, Egypt from My Inside, p. 72.
48. Kermode's interview with Golding, published in *Books and Bookmen*, V (Oct. 1959), p. 10.
49. William Golding, *The Hot Gates*, pp. 95-96.
50. E.L. Epstein, "Golding: Biographical and Critical Notes," *Lord of the Flies* (New York: Capricorn Books, 1959), p. 189.

51. Leighton Hudson, *William Golding, Writers and Critics*, No. 61, (Edinburgh Oliver and Boyd, 1969), p. 38.
52. William Golding, *The Hot Gates*, p. 126.
53. John Haffenden, *Novelists in Interview* (Methuen, London, New York, 1985), p. 106.

The Inheritors

3

Blessed are the Meek: For they shall Inherit the Earth

St. Mathew 5:5

In these words from the Sermon on the Mount, Jesus offers an apocalyptic vision of the triumph of innocence on earth. This phrase "to inherit the earth" is used on a number of occasions in the Bible and each time it is the good, the holy, the meek who are referred to. But if such a splendid state of affairs is to be achieved, a very radical change in the way of the world will have to take place, for experience teaches us it is generally the self-seeking, the aggressive, the ambitious and the ruthless who gain and hold earthly power and property. The values of the late Victorian world, with the emphasis on manufacture and making money, create a war-like society in which there are only those who make it and those who are broken in the process. The world may appear to be making progress by getting and spending, but the reality is a regression from Christian values to the law of the jungle, to the ruthless and greedy thirst for domination which lifted man out of the slime and gave him possession of the world and power over all other creatures.

Golding's second novel *The Inheritors* (1955) is a fable of pre-history which relates the encounter between the last surviving family of the Neanderthal species and the first "true men" as H.G. Well's calls *Homosapiens* in his *Outline of History* and the eventual extermination of the former by the latter. They oust the gentle Neanderthalers with a cruelty and determination which the novelist pits ironically against the optimistic view of "progress" in H.G. Well's *Outline of History*. The group is only a remnant, those who have survived a forest fire; their encounter is with other creatures, men and women, whose existence has till then been unknown to them. Their instinctive reaction to these strangers is one of admiration and affection, but for their part, the humans hate and fear them, killing them on sight. Inevitably they are destroyed. The narrative closes with a last survivor, Lok, in his death-throe, howling in grief for the companions he has lost and for the explicable misery that has possessed him. While at the same time humans row away in their dug-out down the lake. The story is seen from the point of view of the Neanderthalers, and thus summoning up the very origins of speech and sin.

As J.S. Ryan has said the title of this novel would seem to allude ironically to the words of the Beatitude "since it is not the meek who inherit the earth but the killers of the meek."[1] Golding must have had a wry smile on his face when he selected this title, from the novel *The Inheritors* written jointly by Joseph Conrad and Ford Madox Hueffer which was published many years earlier in 1901. It has a similar theme, in that it is concerned with the destruction of one civilization by another. It is, however, at the other end of the time scale and shows our own civilization being over thrown by a race of *Fourth-Dimensionists*. The most significant similarity between the two books is that in each case the new people exert over their predecessors a strange fascination which is akin to love. As Lok, yearns towards the new people "with a terrified love" (p. 191) he remembers:

> Liku looking up with soft and adoring eyes at Tanakil (and guesses) how he had gone with a kind of eager fearfulness to meet his sudden death. (p. 191)

The Conrad-Hueffer novel also seems to direct us back to the Bible, for the heroine of that novel claims that her people are "to inherit the earth." The earth did belong to them once, but when *Homosapiens* arrive, they intended to inherit the earth.

Golding's message like that of Conrad's and Hueffer's, appears to be contradictory: it is the strong and the ruthless who inherit the earth. Any positive force can only be recognised as positive if it is balanced by a similar negative force. In all his novels, Golding highlights man's capacity for evil, his negative driving force. It was this balanced knowledge of good and evil that made *Homosapiens*, the superior race, and so, ironically they, rather than the meek become the inheritors. As Neanderthal man was meek he lacked the necessary cunning and when pitted against a newer race, which was determined to survive whatever the cost, he could not overcome the natural trust of others and so was eliminated. The meek and gentle Neanderthals are slaughtered by our ancestors, who possess the monstrous and brutal qualities of ruthlessness and self-interest which enable them to survive and progress. The price of such progress is terrible. These aspirant humans give us the world as an inheritance, but we inherit also the regrettable qualities.

Golding, in a self-referential phrase calls himself "a propagandist for Neanderthal man."[2] One of his favourite pastimes in his youth was digging for the relics of ancient, people. During one of his amatuerish excavations at a pre-historic site, he came upon the remains of a "family of innocence."[3] But even as he was longingly visualising them, he saw the remains cruelly flung back into the earth and covered by a bulldozer to make a runaway. To the sensitive imagination of Golding, it was suggestive of civilization's arbitrary encroachment upon the primeval regions. He says that it "may very well have been a prehistoric murder."[4] This experience has evidently left its mark on his imagination, for the "pre-historic murder"[5] forms, on the ostensible level, the theme of *The Inheritors*—Liku's sub-sapiens folk representing the "phantom family" and *Homosapiens* who exterminate them taking the place of the bulldozer.

In *The Inheritors* Golding presents the primeval to demolish the view that civilised man is a distinctly superior being. According to the rationalistic concept of the Fall, Adam's apparent act of disobedience is the first significant progressive step; it is the first expression of man's spontaneous activity, the first daring act of reasoning and the most fortunate and greatest event of the human history. We see in this story the progress from instinct to reason. Darwin's theory of evolution placed man at the apex of creation. It equated evolution with progress. The works and findings of these thinkers provoked a strong reaction in writers who are at odds with the whole enterprise of civilization. One such work is *The Outline of History* by H.G. Wells, a staunch Darwinian and rationalist. Well's account of Neanderthal man:

> We know very little of the appearance of the Neanderthal man, but this...seems to suggest an extreme hairiness, an ugliness, or a repulsive strangeness in his appearance over and above his low forehead, his beetle brows, his ape-neck, his inferior stature...says Sir Harry Johnston, in a survey of the rise of modern man in his *Views and Reviews* "The dim racial remembrance of such gorilla-like monsters, with curring brains, shambling gait, hairy bodies, strong teeth and possibly cannibalistic tendencies may be the germ of the ogre in folklore...."[6]

which is used as the ironical epigraph to *The Inheritors*, not only helps to place the novel chronologically but also provides Golding with the base from which to attack the illusions held by modern man about himself encouraged by liberal thinkers like Wells. Golding himself remarked to a BBC commentator, that this was the initial spring board for his own fable about the encounter between the Neanderthals and his immediate descendant Cro-Magnon man.

The Outline does seem at first to have been a source of information for narrative details. The geographical setting as well as the physical characteristics of the two species with some modifications derive from Well's account. But Golding intended another ironic rebuff to 19th century smugness and explicated in an interview the ironic inversion at length:

> Well's *Outline of History* is the rational gospel in excelsis, I should think. I got this from my father, and by and by it seemed to me not to be large enough...to neat and slick. And when I re-read it as an adult I came across his picture of Neanderthal man, our immediate predecessors, as being those gross brutal creatures who were probably the basis of

> the mythological bad man, whatever he may be, the ogre. I thought to myself that this is just absurd. What we're doing is externalising our own inside. We're saying, "Well, he must have been like that, because I don't want to be like it, although I know I am like it."[7]

Such notions only betray, according to Golding, man's "appalling ignorance of his own nature."[8] In fact, the ogre or the beast to recall Simon's words, is only us.

Early criticism tended to see the novel as fairly exciting, pre-history, as pseudo-science fiction, or as bad anthropology. Several anthropologists reluctantly dismiss the book because modern paleontology does not support Golding's picture of Neanderthal man's relation to Cro-Magnon man. Apparently, there is no evidence that the second race exterminated the first and it is more likely that the Neanderthals were over evolved and over specialised for the peculiar conditions of the lake Pleistocene.

Kenneth Rexroth in an article which is consistently malevolent in tone argues that "modern paleontology does not support Golding's picture of Neanderthal man or of his relation to Cro-Magnon Man."[9] Golding's account of the Neanderthal may not have been anthropologically accurate. It differs in some significant points from the accounts given by anthropologist. Louis J. Halle writes:

> ...he (Neanderthal man) represents the beginning of civilized man in the sense that he went in for religious observances, which suggest an intellectual capacity for abstract concepts. It also suggests that he must have had the kind of spoken language we have, if less refined and subtle.[10]

But Golding's Neanderthals are incapable of abstraction and are almost without formulated speech and thought. Golding himself aware of the contradictions said that he had read everything there was to read on Neanderthal man and contradictions which have now emerged may be the result of new evidence."[11]

Kenneth Rexroth goes on to say: "Of course, there is nothing wrong with invention, extrapolation, or anachronism in a novel about Neanderthals, if it can be made convincing."[12] It is convincing and many critics have acknowledged it to be so. Bernard S. Oldsey and Stanley Weinthraub quote from a letter written to them by Prof. B. Harris, a developmental psychologist, acknowledging Golding's achievement in depicting primitive consciousness that "Golding beats all the psychologists in his conceptualization and portrayal of a limited mentality—which is what cultured anthropologists and psychologists would assume about a sub-sapiens level of evolution."[13]

In a writing ultimately, Kenneth Rexroth himself says, "It's the end in view and means employed that count."[14] First, it should be noted that *The Inheritors* is not a novel on Neanderthal man. It is a work of art tracing imaginatively the evolution of human consciousness.

Golding is not concerned with the specific life of Neanderthal man as such, even as he is not concerned with the specific life of his own times. It is something more than an allegorical fable, a mode he regards as being "an invented thing on the surface."[15] He uses the bare realistic details for the purpose of building up a myth of his own. It aspires to the condition of myth, "something which comes out from the roots of things in the ancient sense of being the key to existence, the whole meaning of life, and experience as a whole."[16]

Like *Lord of the Flies* it starts as a simple argument with the smug 19th century doctrine of progress—and proceeds to show, through the tragedy of 'the people' alone, the genesis of the mythological monster in the human skull. It explores the possible origins of man's guilt and violence in the evolutionary appearance of *Homosapiens*, but the fable mythic in impulse, consciously tries to construct a mythopoeia relevant to contemporary man by using anthropological conventions.

The novel is ostensibly the story of the suppression of the Neanderthal man by Cro-Magnon man. The other historical or rather prehistorical dimension with which it is concerned is that of the Fall of Man. It replicates the story of the introduction of sin into the world. It has its source in the story of pre-lapsarian man (man before the Fall) from the first two chapters of

Genesis. It is an expression of the author's belief concerning man's relationship with the Universe and with God the creator. The 'people' belong to that time in the Bible and particularly the account of Garden of Eden. The 'people' are without sin because they have no knowledge of good and evil. It is a paradigm of the human situation repeating itself in the history of man or human species as each taste of the tree of knowledge of good and evil and passes from a state of primal innocence to rational consciousness and guilt. It depicts the natural man in his pure innocence, the loss of this innocence and the tensions and anxieties associated with the loss. It is clearly a theological use of a mythological theme to explain man's progression from a state of innocence and bliss to the present human condition of knowledge of sin, misery and death.

Golding's Neanderthalers are the true innocents, the harmless men, not only without evil themselves but incapable of understanding it when it meets and destroys them. They run to meet their killers in love, and are quite incapable of preserving themselves by destroying their oppressors. We can contrast every aspect of the "fallen" life of the New Men with the "unfallen" life of 'the people' and take home to ourselves the message that comes from realising the nature of our ancestry. We reach a point when the novel seems no longer essentially about Neanderthal man at all, but merely using him as a way of analysing the nature of the Fall. Emblems emerge: the dead tree from which Lok and Fa look down on the destruction of their Eden; the waterfalls which marks the limit innocence, but beyond which the sinful have to travel towards a line of darkness.

Though the novel charts the story of Man's Fall, the whole story suffers a strange dislocation in the hands of Golding. He presents an inversion of God-the-father oriented Christianity. The patriarchal society created by male God or Jehovah in the Bible becomes a matriarchal society created by the female God Oa. There is a relentless logic in the people's religion: the act of creation belongs to woman; therefore the great Oa who was before all things is a woman; from her belly she "brought forth woman," who in turn brought forth the first man out of her belly" (p. 35). Though the superior strength of man is acknowledged so that in physical things he leads and his word guides, only the woman may commune with a woman. Oa, like Jehovah, was and is; Jehovah says, "I am Alpha and Omega, the beginning and the end, the first and the last" (Revelation, 22:13, 21.16). So also she is O and A, Omega and Alpha, the end and the beginning. Oa, their spiritual leader is a feminine synonym for God. Golding makes symbolic use of the primitive material. The fable presents its version of loss of Eden not by a full and rich creation of life but by exactly the opposite technique.

The plot, a dramatic account of the extermination of one species by another, is extremely simple. We follow the imagination of a small band of 'people' (p. 31) from their winter quarters by the sea to their summer quarters in coastal mountains at the edge of a river and waterfall. For a long time the epigraph from Well's *Outline* remains the only clue to the identity of the story's actors. (The band of eight the old man, Mal, the leader of the group; the old woman, keeper of the fire, who has no other name and is always called 'the old woman,' Lok, the main protagonist, extremely simple, even among these simple people. Ha, the other mature man; Fa, Lok's woman companion; Nil, the mother 'the new one'; the baby always called 'the new one'; and finally, Liku, who carries with her a tree root in the shape of a doll, her 'little Oa' or representation of their goddess the great Oa is the only Neanderthal group to have survived a Great Fire). Coming to a marshy stretch of water, they discover a log-bride is missing—an ominous fact since in the past it has always been there and should still remain: "Today is like yesterday and tomorrow" (p. 40) they console themselves. But this faith is to be bitterly shattered. The leader of the band, Mal the old man with all the memories of the sweeter times, falls into the dreaded water. The tribe tortuously climbs up a cliff and is forced to make a new passage at their ancient overhang. They set about finding food, but it gradually becomes clear that for some inexplicable reason Mal has miscalculated the seasons and they have arrived at the summer quarters too early. Then Ha falls victim to some unknown calamity—in swift succession

Mal dies of over exposure, Nil and 'the old woman' are killed, perhaps by some creature, the two children, Liku and 'the new one,' are kidnapped. Only Lok and Fa remain, frantically trying to rescue the children whose kidnapping they simply cannot understand.

The narrative then shifts to the activities of the New People, the starving tribe is gradually introduced the charismatic magician Marlan and the beautiful Vivani, the artist Tuami; Pine-tree, Chestnut-head, Bush, Tuft, the four braves; Twal and her daughter Tanakil. We watch from the summit of the dead tree through Neanderthal eyes the mysterious gestures of this tribe, their mimetic rituals, their rapacious orgies, their terrified brutal efforts to escape from some unknown danger. A last crucial episode occurs at the overhang: the New People are confusedly trying to accomplish the portage of their canoes past the waterfall: "There was a hysterical speed in the efforts of Tuami and in the screaming voice of the old man. They were retreating up the slope as though cats with their evil teeth were after them" (p. 209). Lok and Fa make one last desperate effort to rescue the children, Fa distracting attention so that Lok can rush for the new one. The attempt fails, several of the New People fall over the fall while Tuami draws a savage totemic figure. "It was some kind of man. Its arms and legs were contracted. There was hair standing out on all sides of the head as the hair of the old man had stood out when he was enraged or frightened" (p. 215). A confused scuffle ensues and Fa is chased to a log. The log spills over the cascading waters of the fall and she is carried lifeless over the fall as Lok watches.

What follows the death of Fa is not longer seen through Lok's consciousness, but is third-person account. We watch Lok's dumb pain as he scurries back and forth looking for Liku; finally he unearths Oa-doll and with this, folds himself into a foetal position at the ancient grave in the overhang. We watch him as he prepares himself for death. The 'people' are now extinct. At the fable's close one solitary canoe is seen carrying the tormented New People upward toward some new camp. We now see events through the consciousness of one of them, Tuami. Tuami broods on the change and his bedevilled irrational grief, "as though the portage of the boats...from that forest to the top of the fall had taken them all onto a new level not only of land but of experience and emotion" (p. 225). As he studies the tribe before him, their history is swiftly reviewed. They too have been overcome by water: Tuami thinks, "I am like a pool...some time has filled me, the sand is swirling, the waters are obscured and strange..." (p. 227). And *The Inheritors* ends with Tuami staring out at "a line of darkness" (p. 233) apparently without end.

It takes its plot in large measure from Well's semi-documentary adventure story, 'The Grisly Folk.' And in doing so it reverses the moral values of *Outline of History*. First the moral natures of the two species are exchanged, Wells portrays the Neanderthals as monsters easily conquered by a clever species. Golding's 'people' are a gentle and harmonious tribe, unable to conceive of the New People's violence, rapaciousness and corruption. The novel set up in the last days of Neanderthal species essentially deals with man's violence and the depravity of human nature. It is the innocence of the doomed predecessor that we see enacted, for, until the last pages, we see the activities of the New men, intelligent and so capable of evil, through the bewildered eyes of the old.

The theme of responsibility is central to both the overt and the allegorical meanings of *The Inheritors*. Although Golding depicts the 'people' in a favourable light, he shows Tuami and the New People as viewing them in a Wellsian light. They appear to be neither simple nor innocent but Gorilla-like monsters with cannibalistic tendencies. Their ogre-like qualities seem to justify man in destroying them before he himself is destroyed. Tuami's people kill and destroy because they believe that if they do not they will themselves be killed; "If we had not we should have died" (p. 228). Tuami remarks, as he sails up the river and his mind plays on the events which have preceded their flight. We are left to wonder if it is all the ghastly mistake, a lack of communication which has annihilated Lok and his companions, killed many of the New People, left Tanakil insane and the rest fearful and disturbed. Certainly, the misunderstanding is there, but the cruelty and violence were unprovoked. He was killed without warning. Nil and the old women viciously destroyed though they were clearly defenceless. Liku, a small child, was murdered and eaten. It is only after all these events that Lok and Fa, in trying to rescue 'the new one,' act in a way which could appear to be hostile. Thus, although Tuami's tribe see the people as devils, this is a figment of their imagination. They believe the 'people' to be wild and savage as they are unaware of the true gentleness, kindliness and love to be found amidst their simplicity. 'Civilization' has moved a step forward. The evil is within themselves and man is seen responsible for his own wrong doing.

Tuami and the "inheritors" clearly belong to the world of Fallen Man, like Cain they commit murder. In Genesis 4:8, Cain says to his brother Abel, "Let's go out in the fields" and 'when they were out in the fields, Cain turned on his brother and killed him.' Like Noah who "took one of each kind of ritually clean animal and bird and burnt them whole as a sacrifice on the altar" (Genesis, 8:20) they too offer sacrifices and once again like Noah too, they become drunk (Genesis, 9:21). 'After he drank some of the wine, he became drunk, took off his clothes and lay naked in his tent.'

Only his greed and lust tempt Lok to become one of the New people by drinking the potent honey-mead. The implicit, prohibition against gaining such knowledge is reinforced by Fa's injunction, not to touch it. Lok drinks, knowing that he is disobeying the Oa in her, "not seen but sensed like a cloud round her" (p. 117). The fall is thus accomplished from the evil within Lok. The fallen man in the shape of the New people, learns that there is no serpent.

Though many animals and birds are mentioned, the most significant absentee from Golding's allegory of the Fall is the serpent. Through the serpent, the Biblical myth in the third chapter of Genesis externalises evil. When Adam is blamed for his disobedience he attempts to shrug off the responsibility by blaming Eve; "The women you put here with me gave me the fruit and I ate it", says Adam (Genesis, 3:12) and she in her turn blames the serpent; And the "Lord God asked the Women, why did you do this?" She replied "The snake tricked me into eating it" (Genesis, 3:13). If like Cain, they rise up and slay their brothers they again like Cain, must bear the responsibility themselves.

What is fundamental in Golding's moral scheme is that knowledge makes one participate in responsibility. The guilty may make a darkness, some blank fear or some totem of fear, but knowledge is recognition and it brings with it the necessity to acknowledge in our own nature the Beast. The problem that *The Inheritors*, *Lord of the Flies* and *The Spire* raises is the contemporary gap between such knowledge and that knowledge put into action; the whole impulse of a creature who transforms darkness of the unknown into a threatening ogre, or devil or external system of evil.

With manipulative intelligence comes this capacity to avoid our essential selves, or what lies in our 'darkness'. It is our particular sin to explain away our own shortcomings rather than remedy them. Thus in *The Inheritors* "Lok felt himself secure in the darkness" (p. 155). While the new creatures are terrified of it. To Golding's moral diagnosis—man abstracts from his own evil—something his nature possesses—and projects it as a fear of something other which will haunt or destroy him. As Vivani stands fearfully stroking the new one, whom they regard as a totemic figure, and stoking the fire which is already excessive, they all face "*Outward* at the darkness of the forest" (p. 195). But their Promethean fire itself metamorphoses darkness, makes the island so impenetrably dark that the night-sight of Lok and Fa is temporarily lost. In Lok's mind the fire and the fall become associated so that the clearing below the tree is beaten with a 'fountain of flame' (p. 171), not warm light but 'fierce white-red and blinding' (p. 171). The firelight symbolically intelligence, intensifies the darkness, and in fact makes it hideous. Precisely the same light and dark image is repeated at the fable's close. The New People's canoes sail forward on shining water, namely, water that is imagistically associated with light, yet it also seems hemmed in by darkness. In fact, it projects outwards the moral darkness of the sailors. In the fable's very last line, Tuami is made to remark that "there was such a flashing from the water" that "cannot see if the line of darkness had an ending" (p. 233). Obviously Golding is making by the symbolic extension of optical illusion, the point that intense light, obscures. Man's intelligence projects its own internal darkness outward.

Man's mind, Golding is saying, deceives itself; Man imagines devils who "live in darkness under the trees" (p. 233) and then tries to destroy the fantasies he has himself created. Yet this fear of "tree-darkness" drives man forward—it is, in fact the very basis of his strength, as Lok understands when he knows "the impervious power of the people in the light" (p. 185). "Haunted, bedevilled, full of strange irrational grief," (p. 225) man carries his fear with him. In this investigation into the nature of evil and responsibility Golding returns to a mythical time of innocence, but Paradise seems already lost.

When we first meet Lok's people they are already a long way from the idyllic existence of the Garden of Eden. They suffer hunger and thirst, cold and physical misery and the old man Mal is dying. Mal, tells the others stories of the prelapsarian life "when it was summer all year round and the flowers and fruit hung on the same branch" (p. 35). This is now only a memory, a story to be passed from one generation to another; yet like Adam and Eve in the Garden of Eden the people are naked and not ashamed, which is similar to Adam and Eve in the Garden of Eden: "The man and the woman were both naked, but they were not embarrassed" (Genesis, 2:25).

With the New people the knowledge of evil is introduced. Tuami and the "Inheritors" belong to the world of Fallen Man; like Adam and Eve they cover up their nakedness: "As soon as they had eaten it (the fruit of the forbidden tree) they were given understanding and realized that they were naked; so they sewed fig leaves together and covered themselves" (Genesis, 3:7). The first result of the Biblical Fall is that Adam comes to know fear: "I was afraid" (Genesis, 3:10). Throughout the novel the New people constantly manifest fear and this is communicated to Lok and Fa so that their waking moments are troubled by a "new habit of terror" (p. 170). The inheritors, our ancestors, take the cave men to be devils and flee in terror.

Golding makes use of the Original sin, which is the morally vitiated condition in which one finds oneself as a member of a sinful race. In Genesis, Chapter 3, this is depicted as an inherited consequence of the first human sin of Adam and Eve. Theologians differ as to the interpretation of this narrative, but it is to be agreed that the Original sin, however mysterious its origin and nature may be, arises from the fact that human beings come into the world not as isolated individuals but as members of a corporate race inheriting both good and evil features from its past history.

Traditionally, the origin has been ascribed to the sin, of the first man, with the consequent transmission of his guilt by hereditary to his descendants. From a stasis of calm description at the fable's opening to the frantic and confused dramatic action at its close, the reader comes gradually to experience imaginatively the loss of innocence and the genesis of guilt.

The first four chapters of the novel where we follow the "people" in their movement upstream from their winter quarters to their summer quarters in the overhang, directly adjacent to the fall, are static, propelled not by action but through description, a mode fundamental to the growth of the fable. For what is encountered, by the reader in these chapters—the tree by the clearing where Lok swings Liku, the ice cavern beyond the waterfall, where "the drone of the fall diminished to a sigh" (p. 81), the fall itself with logs slowly descending—these physical phenomena assume a dramatic than a symbolic role as the tale proceeds. As substantial phenomena they are, first of all, points in the actual narrative scene which by introduction and reintroduction during the course of the developing narrative, begin to assume a symbolic import like the island and the Head did in *Lord of the Flies*.

First, Lok's incomprehension is our own incomprehension, then Tuami's doubt is our doubt. In the books central confrontation where Lok sees a "thing" in the water—Golding dramatizes the sudden conjunction of this innocence and its perfect opposite: Consciousness. Reading the moment, in a sense, we actively participate in the first emergence of the mythological ogre in the primitive mind.

Hanging from what will be the tree of knowledge, having already learned a new knowledge from that tree, Lok leans out over the dread water trying to reach out towards the island and the kidnapped Liku. He strains and balances, noticing that the water under him darkens as he stretches forward. Just as his ears hear the water fall the branches begin to bend under him. Gibbering in fright, he smiles and a "Lok-face" (p. 107) come up at him as the water appears to rise. It is the moment when the unknown something dark and autonomous confronts Lok's mind. The entire episode is projected through a technique whereby we are locked in the primitive mind and hence without the interpretation as in *Lord of the Flies* where Simon confronts the Head of the Pig. "Pictures" even fear, disappear, yet he cannot connect the Lok-face with himself; it is simply some dark spectre—released from his mind—and now compulsively, independently, capable of harming him. Lok sees something foreign which we know is also himself, but to him it is a threatening image of "teeth grinding in the water" (p. 108). It gradually fuses with a new terror—the result of the water-fall and its implicit Fall:

> The weed-tail was shortening. The green tip was withdrawing up river. There was a darkness that was consuming the other end. The darkness became a thing of complex shape, of sluggish and dreamlike movement. Like the specks or dirt, it turned over but not aimlessly. It was touching near the root of the weed-tail, bending the tail, turning over, rolling up the tail towards him. The arms moved a little and the eyes shone as dully as the stones. They revolved with the body,. gazing at the surface, at the width of deep water and the hidden bottom with no trace of life or speculation. A skein of weed drew across the face and the eyes did not blink, the body turned with the same smooth and heavy motion as the river itself until its back was towards him rising along the weed-tail. The head turned towards him with dreamlike slowness, rose in the water, came towards his face. (pp. 108-09)

The entire episode seems a radically compressed account of book's theme since it connects the two psychic conditions of innocence and guilt, and shows how the latter emerges from the former as Cro-Magnon man emerges from Neanderthal man.

Lok sees the old woman, like one of the logs that keeps falling off the fall, drifting towards him, in the water from the fall. The body is a nightmarish thing in dark water and its knowing eyes are scraped and affronted by the weed-tails. The eyes sweep across his face, "looked through him without seeing him, rolled away and were gone" (p. 109). The eyes that once saw into the mystery of things no longer have the power in the technological world *Homosapiens* has created. And innocence, which before had been characterized by wholeness, becomes aware of deep water within itself inescapably fragmented from itself and uncontrollable. The encounter results in a psychic fragmentation and the similar confrontation scenes in *Lord of the Flies* which however, bring about psychic unification.

The family of "people" migrate to their spring home and slowly realise that things have changed, slowly discover the encroachments of a tribe of "others" (men). The "people" are not capable of thinking, of abstraction and of forming rational connections. They simply act by instinct and "have pictures", many of which they do not understand. Yet, for all other perceptual and intellectual limitations the 'people' have a code of ethics (they will not kill other animals, though they do eat the meat of animals already killed), a deep and humble sense of their own limitations, and a faith in the divine power and goodness of the earth. In addition, the 'people' enjoy a family life free from fighting, guilt and emotional squabbling. The novel is the process of man, conquering the 'people' capturing or killing them one by one. The last of the 'people' is able to watch man, to understand dimly man's power and victory.

But this last survivor of the 'people' is also able to sense in what ways man is a creature different from the 'people.' He watches man brawl and fight, steal other men's mates, suffer guilt and anxiety, tear himself apart between his real ability and his failure to exceed his limitations. The novel carries the implication that man's unique power to reason and thinking carries with it his propensity towards fear and sin and guilt, towards those qualities that cause him pain and misery. It is the

New men who introduces guilt, crime, suffering and conscious ambition into the world of these creatures of primal innocence.

Professor Kermode has summoned up the major theme admirably; "The price of human consciousness, of technical and linguistic power" he writes, "is guilt...the intellectual superiority which enables this victory is measured by the cruelty and guilt invented in the process. Man, who cooks, makes drawings, alcohol and love, can think; he replaces with language that picture-dialect, guiltless of all abstrating, which the victim used and which is found in *Homosapiens* only on certain pathological conditions."[17] There is a close thematic connection between *The Inheritors* and *Lord of the Flies*. It is clear that it is humanity and humanity alone, that generates evil, and when the New Men triumph, Lok, the Neanderthaler weeps as Ralph wept, for the corruption and end of innocence.

All primary human activities are filtered through the polarised lens of Lok's unfamiliarity; sympathetic hunting magic ritual mimesis (the magician in a stag's head), the use of artifacts such as dug-out canoes; murder, religious offerings, intoxication, the conscious and deliberate pursuit of pleasure in the act of love. Gradually, as he and Fa spy on these strange alien creatures, they too are corrupted. Experience breeds awareness. They drink the alcoholic mead and feed identification with the new folk, only to wake and vomit afterwards. In quick succession they fall victims to the evils of alcohol, lust and physical violence. Lok looks at Fa with new eyes and he also, stumbles on the notion of 'likeness.' "They have gone over us like a hollow log" (p. 198) cries Lok in his agony. "They are like a Winter" (p. 198). From the beginning their triumph is inevitable. Golding ends his story by making the New Men abduct a Neanderthal baby. Corruption is complete, evil and knowledge triumphs. Lok and Fa become anthropological analogues of Adam and Eve, but it is man himself whom Golding identifies with the Serpent, who tempts Lok to eat of the tree of knowledge.

The Inheritors is concerned with both a primitive setting and a primitive people, it takes us back to a time some fifty or sixty thousand years ago. It is concerned with that period of prehistory when man as we know him today was evolving from his ape-like predecessors. The main protagonists of the novel, "the people" are Neanderthal man, not quite apes, not quite humans. The primitiveness of Golding's "people" is difficult to imagine. They are completely ignorant, they keep no animals, grow no crops, they can preserve but not create fire, they have no tools, no weapons, they make no shelters against the elements, but rather sleep in caves or under overhanging cliffs; they have no utensils, even for drinking from; they have no means of transport, even over water, they remain completely naked even in the bitterest weather, their knowledge of sex is vestigial, their language is rudimentary.

Materially, the people possess almost nothing—each of the men carries with him a thorn bush which serves several purposes as the need arises; it is a weapon to be used to scare wild animals such as hyenas; for Mal it is a support to lean on; for the more active, such as Lok it is an aid to balancing when he runs swiftly. Liku always has with her "the little Oa," an old root "worn away at the both ends but preserving the exaggerated contours of a female body" (p. 219). This representation of the 'people's' God the great Oa was an imaginative discovery made by Lok. Their only possession is the fire wrapped in clay and leaves and carefully preserved by the old woman. When Fa tries to envisage shells being used as cups she is unable to carry the thought to its conclusion.

Similarly, the 'people' have a completely undeveloped moral sense; not only are they unacquainted with vice but also unaware of virtue. They are unable to grasp concepts and their survival appears to depend upon mutual solicitude. We have to come to terms with a state in which there is an absolute lack of knowledge, accompanied by the ignorance of good and evil. It is until the New people intrude upon them that they are forcibly made aware of evil.

The "inheritors" are for more advanced: they make encampments and shelters; they can create fire they "manufacture" alcohol; they have primitive cups, they make canoes and navigate both the rivers and the seas; they clothe themselves in skins; they are governed by sexual lust; they are capable of logical thought; moreover they have lost the innocence of their predecessors.

Though the modicum of civilization has given the new people some benefits, it has also brought fear to them and fear has bred in them evil. They are willing and ready to kill in cold-blood and they practice cannibalism. They indulge in the vices of modern life—drunkenness, lust, treachery and greed. The characters, the 'people' and the inheritors can be considered as Man before the Fall (Pre-lapsarian Man) and Man after the Fall (Post-lapsarian Man) or ourselves.

The novel begins in innocence, in the innocent perception of the world that is peculiar to the "people" the Neanderthal tribe. The opening paragraph is all laughter and joyous play; as in *Lord of the Flies* figures emerge from a forest and these figures are again child-like, though their play does not have the sinister undertones of Ralph's enacted machine-gunning of Piggy.

The 'people' are in a number of ways like children when Lok eats the dead ice, an act for which he feels guilty since the people respect and wish to avoid harming anything that lives, he makes excuses and tells little fibs to himself and the world in general in an amusingly child-like way (p. 56). But the child-likeness of the people is without the propensity towards evil so evident in the children of his first novel. In the novel's opening pages, we may suspect that we are observing the childhood of our own race, but unfortunately this is far from being the case. When our own ancestors are encountered they turn out to be anything but innocent: they are unhappy, quarrelsome, wracked by fears and murders. Lok, who knows no evil, completely fails to understand the darkness of the human heart. Here the New People fire a lethal arrow at him: "He looked towards the island, saw the bushes move, then one of the twigs came twirling across the river and vanished beyond him in the forest. He had a confused idea that someone was trying to give him a present" (p. 111). This is a touching innocence such as human childhood could scarcely match. Lok fails to recognise aggression because he has none in him and the lack of that quality makes him vulnerable, in fact makes him doomed.

The flight of the arrow which Lok failed to understand is also difficult for us to understand because of Golding's stylised description. The style makes us to be one with the 'people,' who know no evil, more or less incapable of reasoning, enables us to glimpse the world through the eyes of innocence; but this world of innocence is one that we have lost. The difficulty we experience with the experience is a measure of our falleness. The two worlds—the pre-rational world of Neanderthals man's immediate predecessors, and the rational world of *Homosapiens*, man's ancestors clash, as the novel progress, in the mind of the Neanderthal protagonist, Lok and we discover this rise from the world of *sub-sapiens* to that of *Homosapiens* as the Fall of man from his original state of innocence.

The Neanderthals, as Golding represents them, are self-conscious and innocent. They live in a world characterized by harmony between God, man and nature. They have an ineffable sense of belonging to their world. As they return to their summer quarters, the Neanderthals find that everything the stone, the river, the overhang, and, above all, their deity—has waited for them. Lok pats the dead tree affectionately. Ha and Mal look upon the familiar stone lovingly as if it were one of them. As Mal settles himself against the rock, he touches it "gently as Lok or Ha might touch Fa" (p. 32).

It is thus a bond characterized by mutual love by the world's patient waiting for them and their loving memory of it. Oa, the mother goddess, provides food for them—bulbs, grubs and fat buds. The cavern of ice-woman is their sanctuary. Nature seems to partake of their pleasures and pains, dangers and difficulties. As they manage to cross the water joining the trail, they feel relieved and delighted. And the sun "chose this moment to reappear so that the whole world seemed to share their pleasure" (p. 18). The setting of the sun coincides with the disappearance of Ha over the cliff. Mal reports to the people that she "cannot see him any more...there is no sun on the cliff..." (p. 66). Thus the Neanderthal's world represents a state of perfect harmony between man and the universe. They were so close to nature that their religion taught them not to kill. Even when Fa and Lok find the dead doe, they feel guilty about cutting her up to take back to others as food (p. 54). It is permissible for them to eat meat for sustenance when they are not guilty of killing, but a sense of shame and foreboding lingers. As Lok and Fa tear into the doe, driven by hunger and a primitive instinct for survival, their animal nature takes precedence over their social or spiritual nature. At this point Lok rationalizes. The meat is not really for them, even though they devour it as they dismember the animal. It is for Mal, the patriarch who is ill. This is a complicated, sophisticated rationalization, seeming at first far beyond the ability of the characters. But viewed in terms of Wells' passage, the complications are erased; Wells suggested that primitive man may also have been cannibalistic. If driven by hunger and hard pressed, he would sometimes eat his companions or unhealthy children. Golding has inverted the source. Lok and Fa would never have slain the doe, they would have starved first. Nor would they ever slay another hominoid, though the New Men would not hesitate to do so. The 'people' are natural vegetations, with a keenly developed sense of religious values. If they do not live in a Garden of Eden, they do not occupy a state of prelapsarian innocence. They live without Original sin.

The world of the 'people,' is much less idyllic than an island in the sun. It is a cold, hard and hungry place, where there are evil yellow hyenas and where it is sometimes necessary to tear the guts from a dead deer in order to survive. This is no Garden of Eden, but the vision of the people transforms this harsh world to beauty and wonder, a true earthly paradise. Golding's prose shows us that the people instinctively "see into the life of things," are aware of "the one life within us and abroad."[18] The phrases from Wordsworth and Coleridge describe that sense of **livingness** of things. This sense involves a feeling of belonging, of being at home in and a part of the life of nature, a feeling that is a blessed relief from the habitual isolation and alienation from nature of modern civilized man. This dissolving of the self into a greater whole is restorative of the spiritual well-being of the people.

The cheerful acceptance of life on its own terms characterizes the Neanderthals way of life, its state of prefall consciousness.

"Life was fulfilled, there was no need to look further for food, tomorrow was secure and the day after that so remote that no one would brother to think of it" (p. 61). For them "Today is like yesterday and tomorrow" (p. 47). There is no willing on their part, and hence no striving. When Mal dies, they accept the fact of death in the belief that "Oa has taken Mal into her belly" (p. 91). The solemn acceptance with which they perform his burial rites reveals their characteristic resignation which is much more profoundly and movingly in evidence in Lok when he is tragically isolated. The Neanderthals know no formalisation or rationalisation of their feelings and attitudes. In fact, reason, logic and deduction are unknown to them. When Lok is on guard, he makes an effort to think, but finding it difficult gives up with relief. The presence of the ice-women indicates that the winter is not completely gone. Never before have they seen the ice-women still left in the gully. Yet it never occurs to them that they have returned rather too early. Their mental exertion is seen only when they have "pictures," but they cannot piece them together. Any attempt to reorganise them is abandoned with relief. The pictures are the memories of the past or sometimes a vague idea of what they proposed to do in the present to meet an eventuality. Ha, for example, says, "I have a picture of this stone. Mal used it to cut a branch" (p. 31). Fa says to Lok, "I have a picture of us crossing to the island on the log" (p. 120). Occasionally the people are capable of seeing pictures which are more significant. Mal, confounding in his sick mind the past with the present, sees what might be called an apocalyptic picture of the forest burning. Fa, brooding over the disappearance of Ha, exclaims, "Here is a picture, someone is—other. Not one of the people" (p. 71). Such pictures as these, or the dreams like the one that Lok has of the other pursuing him represent their instinctive forebodings, or reveal their intuitive grasp of reality.

As the people share pictures and feelings, they become one mind or no mind. As they are comfortably installed in the overhand around the fire, "one of the deep silences fell on them, that seemed so much more natural than speech, a timeless silence in which there were at first many minds in the overhang;

and then perhaps no mind at all" (p. 34). It suggests a condition of transcendence of time and space signifying a state of undifferentiated consciousness. On the non-mystic level of experience, it suggests "togetherness," or "peopleness" a state of harmony between man and man. This communal bond not only characterizes their way of life, but is the very essence of life. the strings that bind Lok to Fa, Mal, Liku and the rest of the people "were not the ornament of life but its substance. If they broke, a man would die" (p. 78). Therein lies the tragedy of the Neanderthal protagonist. With the snapping of the communal bond, Lok is left in tragic isolation.

The Neanderthals show involuntary responses such as bristling hair, twitching skin and ears. They are guided by instinct. Lok, though witless amply compensates for it by his keen sense-perception. He "performed miracles of perception in the cavern of his nose" (p. 50). He brings his sense-perception into play while searching for the missing Ha and tracking the New Men. Ha searched the forest with ear and nose for intruders (p. 13).

The language of the Neanderthals has not evolved enough to convey their ideas or thoughts. Where their language fails, they resort to miming, telepathy and gestures. Lok feels aware of his inadequacy to find words to describe the New man and so mimes him.

Allied to the inarticulateness of speech is their innocence of heart. They view the world from a position of absolute trust, one that admits no sense of evil. Lok mistakes the arrow shot at him by the new man for a gift, and never suspects their intention when Lok attempts to take away Liku and the new one without their knowledge, "...the knowledge that they were about to cheat these strange people" (p. 179) fills him with dread. In fact it is not cheating them, but an attempt to rescue the abducted children. This is a clear case of doomed innocence and its problematic character. Far from being cannibalistic, the Neanderthals instinctively shun violence and cruelty. Whereas Jack and his boys in *Lord of the Flies* remorselessly track down a pig and kill it, the Neanderthals have scruples even about touching a dead doe.

In the happy and unfallen Neanderthal world, Mal recalls still better days—a paradisiacal state when "it was summer all year around and the flowers and fruit hung on the same branch" (p. 35). But now as they return to their summer quarters, they are greeted by ominous portents. Today is not going to be like yesterday. They confront events, catastrophic in their nature and implications. In the first instance they return to the overhang too early. It may be attributed to Mal's deteriorating powers. They find the usual log across the marsh water gone. It is a prelude to the ultimate disappearance of the Neanderthal species itself. The hand that has removed the log is to make havoc of the Neanderthal world. It causes the death of their patriarch, Mal. As Fa says, "the log that was not there" killed him (p. 98). Mal, as he nears his end, is filled with nostalgia for their Eden, which he sees to be in danger of vanishing. His people fail to grasp his apocalyptic picture of the forest burning. They have no sense of the impending collapse.

The people have a marked tendency to lie down and die. They are not equipped by nature for survival in this rough world. Besides the smart, go-ahead New people they are not merely innocents but fools. They are much less intelligent than their rivals in terms of practical reason and their generous and trusting nature makes them easy prey, almost willing victims. As in Blake's *Song of Innocence*, the innocent vision is an admirable thing in itself but makes the innocent extremely vulnerable to exploitation or aggression on the part of those whose nature is not free from evil. Ha runs to greet or embrace those who kill him. The people are fools in just this way; their good nature makes them defenseless. The biggest fool among them is the book's central character, Lok.

Lok is quite explicitly a fool. When first we see him he is clowning around and his role in the tribe is that of a buffoon. He makes the others laugh and they are appreciative of that gift. As the novel progress, it becomes clear that his intelligence is far inferior to that of Fa, who shows some ability to reason and to think creatively, to progress, mentally. He is slower to learn than Fa, his innocence harder to penetrate. That innocence is protected by sleep from witnessing the death of Liku and thus he fails to appreciate the outrage and horror which the enormities of the New people inspire in Fa. Ha continues to feel a deadly attraction towards them and to regard them with pity. His feelings for his enemies amounts almost to love.

Lok, like Simon before him, is a holy fool and a Christ-figure. He is the only male of the 'people' to penetrate the mysteries of the patriarchal Oa—religion and he is left at his death with the corpse of the religion in the form of Liku's doll, the "little Oa". The cult of Oa requires respect for all the living creature she created and stands in stark contrast to the religion of the New people in which a cruel god demands blood-sacrifices in order to be placated. Lok and Fa observe such a sacrifice from a "dead tree" a phrase suggestive of the tree upon which the willing and innocent victim Christ was sacrificed. The resemblances to Christ are not confined solely to Lok but extend to others of 'the people': the fall is the cause of Fa's death on another dead tree, Liku is eaten as part of a religious rite of the New people. The innocent nature of the 'people' is Christ like, but it is Lok who is most clearly identified with that meek and willing victim who took the sins and sorrows of man upon himself. Here, left alone, he feels he has become the leader, the whole people, and that he has a wise new head that knows sad new truths.

The new head knew that certain things were gone and done with like a wave of the sea. It knew that the misery must be embraced painfully as a man might hug thorns to him and it sought to comprehend the "new people from whom all changes came" (p. 194). Lok is willing to take the crown of thorns upon himself. He fails, however, to comprehend the 'new people' and they seem equally incapable of understanding him or his kind.

The new people do not give themselves much of a chance to become acquainted with the nature of Lok or his people. They are aliens, thus a threat, thus evil, thus 'forest devils' (p. 224). They project their own darkness, their sins and sorrows, their own propensity towards evil, out into "the darkness under trees" (p. 231) an unwise manoeuvre as in *Lord of the Flies*. These devils must be destroyed or placated. The new people, terrified by the nocturnal raid of Lok and Fa which intended no harm to them, leave gifts for the devils and ultimately are prepared to sacrifice to them the child Tanakil. Lok and Fa have no device for such blood sacrifices. They set free the child and run towards the new people bringing proof of their innocence. But the new people, in no state to understand, recover their own and repel them, fatally injuring Fa, who drifts back over the fall, and condemning Lok to a death of lonely agony. It is the end of the 'people.' Their Christ-like qualities make them unfit for survival in a world of Darwinian survival of the fittest. They are triumphantly innocent. They cannot get past the fall. But this innocence makes them natural victims. They come with Tanakil offering freedom, but the new people are taking no risks. They are concerned merely to defend their own interest and get on in the world; in order to do so they are prepared to reject and crucify Christ. That would seem to be the high cost of gaining the whole world. The unattractive description of Neanderthal man is soon forgotten, in the engaging character of Lok. The physical details of his appearance, the chestnut curls that lie "on his neck and down his spine" seem to have little in common with the "extreme hairness" and "repulsive strangeness" of the being Well's describes. It is not until chapter eleven that this primitive being emerges again with a full description in Golding's own words of Lok the Neanderthal man:

> a strange creature, smallish and bowed. The legs and things were bent and there was a whole thatch of curls on the outside of the legs and the arms. (p. 219)

As a source book Well's *Outline of History* does help in placing the novel chronologically but Golding interprets history on his own terms; Lok's people are not monsters, with cannibalistic tendencies, they are simple, active people, kind and gentle and far from being cannibals. The evil attributed to them is seen in the minds and imagination of "the inheritors."

Fa, Lok's male, accompanies him in most of his expeditions. Fa, is the most intelligent of the people. Her mind plays with possibilities, though she rarely has the capacity to develop them. It is she, who tries to invent a container for drinking from, even if it is only a sea shell. She understands the use of arrow which

Lok calls a "twig." "We throw stones at the yellow ones," she comments (p. 119). Her ingenuity is most stretched, when she is making plans for rescuing the new one from Tuami's people.

When Fa and Lok discover the New people's mead, it is Fa who knows that they should not touch it and Lok who tempts her. Nevertheless, it is Fa, again who realises the potential of a drinking vessel and raises the pot to her lips; Lok bends down and sips. There's a curious parallel to this incident in the Bible, in the seventh chapter of the Book of Judges when God directs Gideon to choose as battle—ready the three hundred men who lap water from their hands and to reject those who bend down on their knees beside the stream to drink. If they are pre-Lapsarian men their gentle kindness has gained them no reward. Their God has neglected to maintain "the herb yielding seed, and the fruit tree yielding fruit" (Genesis, 1:11). Already the beasts of the forest prey upon each other and in their turn the 'people' must protect themselves from the ravages of wild cats and other savage animals. Yet there are certain taboos which they do not break as much from custom as from fear. The chief of these appears to be that they should not kill for all living things were Oa's children and the fruit of her belly. In eating the meat of the doe killed by the cat they attempt to justify themselves and Lok in particular suffers agonies of guilt as he holds in his nostril "the rich smell of meat and wickedness" (p. 54).

It is basically a lack of knowledge, coupled with timidity and extreme gentleness, that keeps the 'people' innocent. They are not hunters partly because they have no suitable weapons and partly because they obey blindly a tribal law which they do not really understand. The law is against killing but they fear it may cover the eating of meat as well, and when he is about to die Mal gives them specific warnings against cannibalism. "Do not open my head and my bones. You would only taste weakness" (p. 87). But later when Lok and Fa go into the camp deserted by the new people and see the offerings of stag-meat and honey-drink left for the gods, they no longer feel reluctance or guilt at eating meat, they are soon "tearing at the present, ripping apart the muscle and cramming the raw meat into their mouths" (p. 189). Only when they are "skin tight with food," having succumbed to the sin of gluttony, do they turn their attention to the meat; in quick succession they fall victim to the evils of alcohol, lust and physical violence. Throughout this scene the world 'fall' is repeatedly insistently like a symbolic drum beat:

> The fall was roaring in the cleaning, inside Lok's head.... They were weeping and laughing at each other and the fall was roaring in the clearing...there was nothing but sunlight and the voice of the woodpigeons over the drone of the fall. (pp. 202-04)

During this time the Fall has come to pass, Lok and Fa are no longer innocent, they have the knowledge of evil and have in addition committed evil, Lok is able to say "I am one of the new people" (p. 204). Lok has become fallen Man.

In the chapters depicting the fragmentation of Lok's self, images of darkness abound. The "black changing shape," the "dark island" and "the deadly water" (p. 79), "the ponderous fall" (p. 80) and "the dead tree" (p. 79) are the iterative images that reinforce the sense of the Fall. They acquire a cumulative force in the concluding image of "the line of darkness" (p. 233) apparently without end. To Tuami it is suggestive of the "world of confusion" (p. 231).

Now their Edenic world is invaded by the other. Lok and Fa like Adam and Eve, are tempted to seek knowledge of the other made up of good and evil, and in the process they experience a Fall, a close resemblance of the theme to the Fall myth. Ha runs after another and is killed. Lok's frantic search attracts the new men to the overhang where they kill the old woman and Nil, and abduct Liku and the new one (Nil's baby boy). Thus, there is total dismemberment of the world of innocence wrought not so much by the new people as by the fateful curiosity of the Neanderthals themselves, a temptation that brings them into contact with the corrupt consciousness and infected will of the other.

In contrast with that of the Neanderthals the world of *Homosapiens* is full of violence, lust, cruelty and superstition.

On the rational level they are superior to the Neanderthalers but on the moral level the new men are far inferior to them. All their new thoughts and gadgets have not altered man's anarchic ways. The atrocities of the twentieth-century are only a re-enactment of the deeds of Tuami's men on the colossal scale and it is these aggressive men who inherit the earth and not the meek as Christ prophesied.

The new people gain the world by disinheriting the meek. They disposes the people, wrench the land from them. Their whole attitude to the world and to each other is inimical, violent and alienated. We discover them encamped on an island, guarding themselves against the world outside. Lok describes them later as "a people of the fall" (p. 195). Their fallen state, their lack of innocence make them also an island people, cursed with a bunker or a larger mentality, cut off by mistrust, fear and aggression from nature and from one another. Among the new people each man is an island. They have lost that sense of belonging in a living world of mother Nature (Oa). They are not able to "share a picture" for the new people do not have the 'peoples' gift of sharing ideas or images, a mark of their extraordinary closeness, intimacy and unity. The minds of the 'people' are closed to each other and their distrustful and wary of one another. "It is bad to be alone. It is very bad to be alone" (p. 196), Lok remarks after his temporary loss of Fa, with the new people.

He is the first victim of the new men. While following them, he disappears over the cliff and is killed. The men raid the overhang while Lok is away, and leave behind a trail of violence and bloodshed. They kill Nil and old women and abduct Liku and the "new one." Fa and Lok the two survivors, are greatly affected by the calamity. They catch a glimpse of the new men from the rock face looking down at the island which happens to be the place of their sojourn, and which for the Neanderthals, is as remote as the moon. To reach the island the people would have to leap the gap between the terrace and the rocks across water that was eager to snatch them over the fall. Only some creature more agile and frightened would dare the leap. So the island remains unvisited (pp. 40-41). It has remained a forbidden place for them, like the forbidden fruit in the Garden of Eden. Now in an effort to regain the new one and Liku, Fa and Lok "dare the leap" and, crossing to the island, find themselves on the threshold of a new experience.

Whereas Fa senses an imminent danger in the new men even at the first encounter, Lok finds them enigmatically attractive. "The undefinable attraction of the new people" (p. 135) and the picture of Liku so maddeningly present (p. 183) drive him again to the bushes at the edge of the water. He runs towards the new way on the island so excitedly that "Fa shared his picture" (p. 135). They do not cross to the island this time, but then they cross the Rubicon. They climb the dead tree, the tree of knowledge. They have a close look at the other made up of good and evil, and find themselves, as the old woman feared, "enmeshed, exalted and tormented" (p. 92).

Lok is fatally attracted to the other even before he sees them. Lok's first glimpse of the new man produces a terribly strange sensation in him. As he traces the other, he is beginning to parody him unconsciously. He tells Fa, "with the scent of the other I am other" (p. 97). The strangeness and power cannot be resisted. "He was beginning to know the other without understanding how it was that he knew" (p. 77). He is so much obsessed with the other that he feels alienated:

> He was cut off and no longer one of the people; as though his communion with the other had changed him, he was different from them and they could not see him. The other had tugged at the strings that bound him to Fa and Mal and Liku and the rest of the people. (p. 78)

All this, his premonitary dream of the other chasing him (occurring before Lok's actual confrontation with the other) show Lok in a condition of unconscious fragmentation. The arrival of the New Men precipitate the Fall. Theodore Reik[19] mentions the view that the grain of evil was in Adam before he was tempted. It was if not the source, the cause of Fall. Lok's attempts to "comprehend the new people" (p. 194) produces in him sudden flashes of awareness only to leave him in a mystifying darkness. In one of his moments of illumination,

"Lok discovered 'like'" (p. 194). He begins to realise the thrill of what it is to think and avidly employs the newly acquired faculty to comprehend the ways of the New Men. But soon he relapses into the usual incomprehension that characterizes the people, "and then he was Lok again" (p. 195).

Lok vascillates between hope and fear, comprehension and confusion—hope not only to see the New people but to be one of them, fear of the men and fear for his people. Oscillating, between his fascination for the new men and his attachment to his own people, Lok experiences a division within himself. As they watch the New men from the dead tree, Lok feels the division much more strongly, "Now more clearly than ever before there were two Loks, outside and inside. The inner Lok could live for ever. But the outer that breathed and heard and smelt and was awake always was insistent and tightening on him like another skin. It forced the knowledge of its fear, its sense of peril on him long before his brain could understand the picture" (p. 141).

What occurs here is a disfunction between the perceptual world without and the spirit within.

Defining man's nature in terms of fundamental contradiction originating in what he calls the biological dichotomy between missing instincts and self-awareness, Erich Fromm states clearly man's existential predicament:

> Man is the only animal who does not feel at home in nature, who can feel evicted from paradise, the only animal for whom his own existence is a problem that he has to solve and from which he cannot escape. He cannot go back to the prehuman state of harmony with nature, and he does not know, where he will arrive if he goes forward. Man's existential contradiction results in a state of constant disequilibrium.[20]

As the tale unfolds itself, one sees three stages in the evolution of consciousness. The Neanderthal's primordial state of being, "the mindless peace of their accord" (p. 38) may be regarded as the undifferentiated consciousness. In such a state, man is at home in the universe. The second stage is the gradual emergence of self-consciousness, the distinguishing trait of *Homosapiens.* Lok can be seen as a link between the two tribes. His agonizing experience—the feeling of strangeness and terror and the "convulsion of the understanding" (p. 94)—is the primal breach in man's original spirit. The effects of fragmentation are an evidence in the society of the new men: the loss of innocence and of wholeness and spontaneity, infected will and a terrible sense of responsibility and guilt. The new men disposes the Neanderthal of their habitat; they inherit the earth but find themselves a disinherited race. They suffer an attenuation of senses and a deprivation of inner harmony. All this leads to the fall from existential harmony into existential chaos.

The break-up of the inner unity that characterizes the primordial state of being is paralleled by the end of the Ice Age. To the Neanderthals the Ice Age is the golden age, and its end marks the end of their paradisiacal state. The cataclysmic changes on the macrocosm are thus reflected in the microcosm.

The last chapter switches to a consideration of the state of fallen Man—what Lok has become, what the new people are, what we ourselves cannot escape from being. Now we realise the extent of the new people's terror. In the darkness and strangeness of the mountains and forests, far from their own homeland they had been afraid and had tried to rationalise their fear. Outside, on the trees there were creatures who were seen one moment and the next moment had vanished. In their imaginations Lok and the people were devils; they seemed a threat to the very lives of Tuami and his comrade. In a mad orgy of evil, of sacrifices to the gods, of drunkenness and lust, of murder and cannibalism, they fought against their fear by fighting against the shadows that surrounded them. They finally fled, unaware that they had completely exterminated the inhabitants of the upland forests. But now, far from the mountains, they are still afraid. Tuami reflects that they are what they had been in the gap, "haunted, bedevilled, full of strange irrational grief" (pp. 224-25). What he is learning is that evil is not something outside that can be combated with weapons but it is within man. "What else could we have done?"

(p. 227) he cries, knowing that there were other things they could have done, that they had the choice. Tuami has to come to terms with the significance of the Fall, to learn that it is enacted every time man chooses to follow the evil inside him. Thus, the episode in the mountains represent a re-run of the Fall for Tuami as well as for Lok. When the new people "sailed up the river towards the fall," they were "bold hunters and magicians" (p. 231), now they are morally crushed, for they have submitted themselves to darkness and to evil. Will they, he wonders, have to pay for this when the new one, "the little devil," grows to maturity?

The world of *Homosapiens* too experiences an upheaval. The visitation of their camp by Fa and Lok terrorises them. As they leave the island in panic, they suffer casualties, some of them are carried to their deaths in the stream. Tanakil loses her sanctity while Tuami has a disquieting experience.

> ...they were what they had been in the gap haunted, bedevilled, full of strange irrational grief.... It seemed as though the portage of the boat...from that forest to the top of the fall had taken them on to a new level not only of land but of experience and emotion. The world with the boat moving so slowly at the centre was dark amid the light, was untidy, hopeless, dirty. (pp. 224-25)

Convulsed by the recent events, Tuami who has been sharpening the blade of an ivory dagger which he intends to plunge into Marlan's heart, exclaims, "What was the use of sharpening it (his sword) against a man? Who would sharpen a point against the darkness of the world?" (p. 231). It is the dagger which gives him a new understanding.

So he abandons the dagger and watches the new one crawl over Vivani, the sight of these two together him realise that right choices can be made: atleast they had not killed this baby who seems to hold out a hope of reconciliation.

The boat sails on, and the novel comes to a conclusion with Tuami at last able to sink into sleep. Behind him, both literally and metaphorically is the fall, but the darkness is still present, kept at bay by the "frightened angry love" of Vivani for the "little devil." The waters of time continue to flow and the boat travels with them, but it is not apparent whether the darkness has an ending. The novel seems to be an extended allegory. Not of the fall alone, but of the life of man. It offers for consideration the possibility of ultimate redemption if there is an end to "the lines of darkness." He looks at the line of darkness wondering if it has an ending. The loss of their sense of unity with the universal order prompts the new men to view their environment with suspicion and fear. The inner chaos is projected on the environment, the new men inherit not only the earth, but the "baby devil" which becomes a symbol of their dark fears. They can neither do away with it, nor can they reconcile themselves with it. In the words of Gabriel Josipovici:

> To be born a new man is to inherit a new consciousness and that consciousness will always be aware dimly of the darkness beyond. But, being aware of it, man turns into an enemy, into that which is evil.... Once again Golding revealed not just the under side of civilization, but the negatives upon which civilization itself, but the negatives upon which civilization itself is built. Having experienced what Lok has experienced we can now see more clearly both the necessary triumph of the New Men and its inevitable cost.[21]

The novel questions by implication the primacy of thought over feeling, reason over instinct, and hints at the enormous cost at which man has acquired superiority in consciousness. As Sammy Mountjoy in *Free Fall* states, "consciousness and guilt go together."[22] Man's rational world is characterised by the ironic affinity between consciousness and guilt. Josipovici observes that the world of the new man is an illustration of the observations of thinkers like Freud and Nietzsche that greed, envy and lust are the inevitable concomitants of the civilization. He quotes Freud as saying that negation, language, thought and civilization all go together.[23] The rational man has acquired knowledge which is mainly utilitarian, analytic and dissociated. The analytic intellect is achieved at the expenses of primitive spontaneity and wholeness. The utilitarian and dissociated knowledge of the new men contrasts a kind of wisdom. "...Mal was wise," and the old woman "so close to Oa, knowing so indescribably much, (is) the doorkeeper to whom all secrets were open" (p. 61). The worship of Oa is based on their instinctive awareness of the oneness of all existing things, and contrasts with the ritualistic religion of the new men. The new men are addicted to child murder, violent and lustful orgies and the practice of magic. Their superstition enslaves them to Marlan, the witch doctor of the totemic cult of the stag. The simple offering made by Fa to propitiate Oa contrasts with the people's murder of Liku. It ninverts Well's picture of Homosapiens as a superior being and the Neanderthals as cannibals.

Consciousness brought man individual freedom and responsibility. But it is at once a blessing and a curse. Drobzhansky states, "Man knows that he is accountable for his acts, he has acquired the knowledge of good and evil. This is a dreadfully heavy load to carry. No other animal has to withstand anything like it. There is a tragic discord in the soul of man. Among the flaws in human nature this one is far more serious than the pain of childbirth."[24] It is man's tragic destiny to endure the burden of knowledge.

Though man's rise to consciousness has ensured his survival and contributed to his progress in the evolutionary scale, Golding sees it as a Fall. Man is alienated from his true self on the one hand and from the universe on the other. Thus, the Descent of Man as propounded by Darwin is here inverted and interpreted not only literally, but in the theological sense of the Fall.

The point of view adopted by Golding admirably brings out the Neanderthal's natural pattern of existence. It is difficult to absorb the whole situation as we watch through the eyes of Lok who "gazed without thought" (p. 40) or "looked without seeing" (p. 40). Hence, often we find that "there were questions but no answers" (p. 140). The activities of the new people seen through the eyes of Lok are no better than a puzzling silent film. We, like Lok, see the new men talk, but never hear them. It is difficult to see what it is all about. But then that is as it should be, the "incomprehension" is the thing, it is the Neanderthal way of life. The whole narrative pattern is so devised as to dramatize Neanderthal's man's way of life in his own terms, to present it through the consciousness of the Neanderthal protagonist so that the readers have a feeling that they are not merely watching the Neanderthal world from outside, but are well inside it, as much bewildered, dismayed and appalled as Lok himself. It is not a representation but a communication of innocence. The pattern carries the meaning.

The story is filtered to us through the consciousness of Lok. There is a certain amount of objective narration, but this is kept to a minimum and is reserved for comment on Lok himself. We do not see what Lok has not seen. Thus in chapter two, when the rest of the people are asleep and Lok is left on watch we patrol the terrace with him and as he finally sinks into sleep we are no longer aware of the nights secrets. The chapter ends with a brief objective comment from the narrator, "...Lok was asleep." In later chapters when the people separate and go about their different duties the story always follows the fortunes of Lok. It is the food seeking expedition by Lok, Fa and Liku which is described in chapter three, of the disastrous search for wood in which Ha disappears we know nothing until Nil tells the rest what has happened. Similarly when the people's encampment is sacked, Nil and the old women killed and Liku and the new one kidnapped, the reader learns of the events only as Lok learns of them through the desperate, panic stricken screams of Liku as she is carried across the river and the sight of the old woman's body revolving in the water. The death of Liku is not observed by Lok and therefore not made explicit to the reader. Only through Fa's reactions and the subsequent absence of Liku is the reader able to piece together the story of Liku's end, to understand how the old man's life is saved by the substitution of Liku and to suspect the cannibalism which results in there being nothing left of Liku but a "small white bone." The madness of Tanakil and her horror at the sound of Liku's name support such an interpretation.

It is not until two-thirds of the way through the penultimate chapter eleven that the objective narration fully re-asserts itself and we see Lok through twentieth-century eyes. He is now described as a "red creature" an 'it' and the similarity to Well's Neanderthal man becomes apparent:

> It was a strange creature, smallish and bowed. The legs and thighs were bent and there was whole thatch of curls on the outside of the legs and arms. The back was high and covered over the shoulders with curly hair. Its feet and hands were broad and flat, the great toe projecting inwards to grip. The square hands swung down to the knees. The head was set slightly forward on the strong neck that seemed to lead straight on to the row of curls under the lip. The mouth was wide and soft and above the curls of the upper lip the great nostrils were flared like wings. There was no bridge to the nose and the moon-shadow of the jutting brow lay just above the tip. The shadows lay most darkly in the caverns above its cheeks and the eyes were invisible in them. Above this again, the brow was a straight line fledged with hair; and above that there was nothing. (p. 219)

The apparently objective narration of the chapter eleven shows us a creature primitive in the extreme; the tone however, is in keeping with the earlier part of the book, for we watch Lok weep as he holds in his hands the two mementoes of his beloved Liku; we experience sharply the despair, when, alone, all he has cared for gone, he lies down to die. We are left to comprehend the enormity of the horror which brought him to this state and to anticipate his animal like end as the hyenas sit and wait beside his motionless body.

After the objective interlude in chapter eleven which describes Lok's end there is a shift of focus in chapter twelve. The remaining events of the story are seen through the eyes of Tuami, one of the new people. Golding shows us that life continues with the new people—*Homosapiens*. Man—but it is the life of the post-lapsarian man with his wickedness and guilt. Tuami and his tribe have destroyed their predecessors whom they believed to be "devils" but have not destroyed evil. We realize that it was out of their fear, out of their own inner darkness that they committed the acts which led to the complete annihilation of the innocent people. As their boat takes them away from the mountains and trees Tuami and his tribe are trying to escape from the hell of death and destruction which they have left behind them; they are haunted by their own imaginings. In their minds Lok's people are monsters and the new one, whom they still have with them is seen as a "devil." Tuami aware of the savagery that has been committed is obsessed by guilt; it is expressed in two despairing sentences, "what else could we have done?... If we had not we should have died" (p. 227).

As this chapter unfolds, the loss of simplicity and of innocence becomes more apparent. Tuami sees a change in one after the other of his people. Tanakil has a new life, not her own; Twal, though younger than he, has the body of an old woman; Marlan suddenly appears to be a devil: "...Marlan was red. His arms and legs were contracted, his hair stood out and his beard, his teeth were wolf's teeth and his eyes like blind stones" (p. 22). Even Tuami himself has lost his manhood and is "a changed Tuami." But the novel does not end in despair. The new one's antics and Vivani's fearful love offer hope. The darkness within man, like the darkness outside may remain but it does not engulf him completely.

The sudden shift towards the end pulls us out of the consciousness of Lok and places us outside the narrative at the vantage point from where we can have an objective view of Neanderthal man and *Homosapiens*, and form our own conclusion. The distancing enables us to see Lok as the ape-man as "the red creature" (p. 217). The use of "it" to refer to Lok apparently dehumanizes the character. But it has, in reality, the effect of intensifying our sympathy for Lok, and emphasizing the inhumanity of the "true" men. His cup of sorrow is full when he senses that Liku has been killed and eaten by the new men and it is this realization which hastens his end. It is also a profound moment of revelation to the reader. It completes the inversion of Wells' account of Neanderthal man, and shows our ancestors the *Homosapiens*, as the real cannibals.

James Gindin writes disapprovingly of the shift in point of view in most of the novels and calls it a "gimmick." According to him, it "breaks the unity without adding relevant perspective."[25] The shift of the point of view, far from being a "gimmick" serves to confirm our impressions about *Homosapiens* which have been vague and shows that the world of *Homosapiens* is as convulsed as the world of Lok. This technique, consistently employed in his novels, seems to have been adopted by Golding out of the conviction that the ability to see as many points of view as possible is the way to get at the totality of experience. The switch in point of view lays bare emotional complexities in the lives of the new people—their consciousness and guilt, their self-deceptions and an apprehension of the darkness apparently without end. Samuel Hynes succinctly sums it up: "...we observe as Neanderthal man observes, but we interpret as rational, fallen man interprets."[26]

The point of view is thus employed to depict the cosmic evolution from people to Men, from pre-lapsarian to post-adamite, from a primitive to contemporary mentality. Not only does the reader's mentality emerge from Lok's mind to Tuami's it comes with the Neanderthal's to the "place of the Fall"; it leaves with *Homosapiens*. From the point of view of innocence, the biological evolution is a moral devolution, as ironic a turning as the Well's epigraph or the Beatitude referred to in the title that the 'meek shall inherit the earth.' The departure is a departure from innocence; the light of dawn that touches humanity, like the new spring and new age that the melting ice hails, seems essentially bleak.

The total effect of *The Inheritors* is to implicate the reader in the experience of and responsibility for this loss of innocence; in this way the fable's ideographic structure forces the reader to know that the innocence lost is our own innocence. We proceed within the innocent's consciousness until the penultimate chapter were, after the objective anthropological transition, we enter the New People's minds. This brings pain for the knot binding the people together "by a thousand invisible strings" (p. 104) has been supplanted by the "strips of skin" (p. 208) tying the groaning men to their log/canoes and by the "long pieces of skin" (p. 159) which leashes Liku to Tanakil. And in the fragmentation between inside-Lok and outside-Lok which so intensifies his alienation both from himself and Fa and recognize the very usage of our own dissociated and pluralized sensibilities. The change to Cro-Magnon man's point of view, with its gain in intellectual grasp and apprehensive imagination, involves the painful loss of Neanderthal man's intuitive of disconnected thinking.

It's ideographic structure pictures both man's guilt consciousness and his innocence. We share Lok's disconnected 'picture' for most of the time and then see him from the outside as a grotesque red creature. The focus shifts to the newer tribe and the final objectification of Lok is meant to distance him from us at the same time as winning enormous sympathy for his dying. Later our sense of Tuami is also modified. The effect is to deliberately complicate the possibility of us choosing between two communities: the sensuous innocence of the subhuman and the intellectual guilt of the human one so that the reader experiences the sense of loss and gain together. By means of this structure, point of view and symbolic episodes such as the confrontation scene the reader encounters dark and light, moving beyond simple experience, guilt or simple innocence and love to an idea of the possibility of reconciliation of good and evil.

The settings are used to show that, despite our veneer of civilization we have not learned to combat death and decay; they are all around us and the outward corruption symbolizes man's inner corruption. *The Inheritors*, set in prehistoric times, we expect the settings to be wild and primitive; we are warned very early in the novel, that they are not paradisiacal and that Lok and his companions are not living in a Garden of Eden. The missing log which had been used as a bridge is pictured by Lok as grey and rotting, the water which they had to pass over is a horrible stretching, which extends into a wilderness of unpassable swamp, thicket and bog. In chapter one when the people have crossed the water, they come at last to a clearing. There is the standing corpse of a tree, it is covered in fungi, "plates that stuck out and were full of rain-water, smaller jelly-like blobs of red and yellow, so that the old tree was dissolving into dust and white pulp" (p. 22). As they make their way along the path there is still an overhang of ice left above it and the water that drips down is described as "deadly".

The people too are decaying. The old woman has "withered breasts" (p. 14). Mal's hair is thin and scanty; he has "wrinkled skin" and his eye-hollows are "deep and dark and the eyes in them dull and full of pain." "Life" we are told "had stripped him" (p. 36). Even among the new people Tanakil's mother crumpled; while resting they look flat as dead men.

Not only is there an emphasis on death and decay but some of the language has more positive connotation with evil. There is considerable emphasis on darkness. From the path Lok looked across the "sheer mountain that was black and hidden from the sun" and as they neared the terrace he could see "the forest...already dark behind him" (p. 29). The island where the new people have their camp is total darkness and just before he espies the first of the new people Lok pictures the leap that would have to be made "over the deadly water to the dark island" (p. 79). When he and Fa reach the island and look at the new people they see that branches of trees have been women "so that they made caverns of darkness on either side of the fire" (p. 128). In the final chapter it is from the dark that Tuami and his companions are trying to escape but the book ends with the "line of darkness" still in view.

Periodically throughout the novel darkness and blackness are relieved by fire light. One of the people's recurrent pictures is that of the forest burning, an event stamped upon their memory and dating from Lok's childhood. Under control, the fire is a welcome comfort but the time when the fire flew way and ate up all the trees was a time of fear. The fire is also presented with even more evil connotations. The most striking instance of this is to be found just after Fa has witnessed the death of Liku when what seems to be a positive hell-fire accompanies the orgy of horror in which the new people indulge: "There was nothing warm and comfortable about this fire—it was like the fall, like a cat...the flames...were being squeezed from below, they were red and yellow and white...not warm light but fierce, white-red and blinding" (p. 171).

The depiction of the new people themselves has clear affinities with the medieval picture of hell: "The people were like the fire, made of yellow and white..." (p. 171).

The brooding evil present in the novel is made explicit through the choice of vocabulary. The book's message is underlined when Tuami and his people finally sail away from the scene of carnage they have created. Tuami looks "back at the gap through the mountain and (sees it) full of golden light and the sun was sitting in it" (p. 228).

After all he is not escaping from the dark, but from the light; he now recognizes the evil within him, "strange things... creeping out of the cracks and crannies (of his) mind" (p. 227). Though he has seen Lok's people as devils, though the 'new one' is known as "the little devil," Tuami acknowledges that "the mist," "the sand" are in his own mind.

The world of the new people is essentially our world. We are their inheritors. The new people will go to any length, pay any price including consigning their child to the devil-in order to get on, to gain control of the world. We have control of the world, but the price paid by our ancestors for our position was very high, so high that our triumph seems both empty and precarious. Its emptiness has seen sufficiently outlined in the new people's alienation and fear. Its precariousness derives from their fractiousness and greed combined with their environment. In order to gain ascendancy over other creatures and control of the environment it was necessary for our ancestors to inherit weapons and use them aggressively on prey and potential rivals. But the tendency to identify others as rivals and the violence were inevitably directed towards other humans. The new people are already a splinter-group and the seeds of further violent division are clearly present. That aggression and paranoia combined with weapons of ingenuity, have produced a situation today where at any movement we can destroy ourselves and our world completely.

The association of the new people with the destruction of the forest suggests another way in which the new people might serve us a warning to us of the dangers which, largely as a result of our success, beset us. It is with the publication of *The*

Inheritors that awareness has become widespread of the threat that man poses to himself and to other forms of early life by his increasing ability to alter the nature of the environment in the pursuit of gain. Golding, the prophet shows admirable foresight here. Today man is highly destructive of the world's tropical and equatorial forests, home to an immense variety of flora and fauna and also a source of much of the world's oxygen. Here again progress means destruction of others and progress towards self-destruction. Today man can build a great highway through the forests of the Selvan, the great Amazonian forests. There is a great tribute to his determination to gain control of all the earth but also a spectacular instance of his tendency to treat trees merely as green things that stand in the way. The new people's progress already shows this tendency to change and mar that face of the nature, to crush without thinking the life that goes in the way:

> The trail had changed like everything else that the people had touched. The earth was gouged and scattered, the rollers had depressed and smoothed a way broad enough for Lok and Fa to walk abreast.... Fa looked mournfully at his face. She pointed to a smear on the smoothed earth that had been a slug. (p. 198)

The shrinking of the great forests of the tropics threatens the existence of higher creatures than slugs, endangers the existence of the great apes, whom we now know to be no fierce forest devils but affectionate, intelligent and gentle giants reminiscent of Lok, and threatens the existence of also primitive human cultures. The behaviour of the new people seems sadly our prophetic of our indifference to the fate of our positive hostility towards those identified as outsiders, aliens or primitives. A catalogue of human crimes resulting from such hostility would be long. The new people have a laager or bunker mentality: they feel that whatever is outside of them poses a threat to them. They are in a grip of a paranoia. Such paranoia, such readiness to defend the tribal laager by attacking those supposed to be a threat, may be the end of all us. This self-protective and self-advancing aggressiveness towards outsiders leads the new people to commit genocide. They wide Lok's race from the face of the earth, just as an attempt was made to exterminate the Jewish race, a race identified by Hitler, as a threat to the progress of civilization and the all-round bogey men of history, the sort of role Well's gives to the Neanderthal men in the epigraph to the novel. The 'people' are, indeed, at certain moments reminiscent of the Jews, as when Mal gives an account of their genealogy right back to a sort of Garden of Eden and, most poignantly, when Lok and Fa give expression to their feelings about the disastrous encounter with the new people in words which in their stark simplicity and power recall the verses of the Psalms or the Lamentations of Jeremiah. "They have gone over us like hollow log. They are like a winter" says Fa, pointing to the crushed slug" (p. 198). With regard to primitive people even our best intention seem to have disastrous consequences. Expeditions leave gifts in jungle clearing to establish contact with the primitive tribes, but once contact with civilization is established the influence upon the tribe is generally baleful, leading to the collapse of the tribe's whole culture and way of life. The new people too leave gifts for the forest devils, including the "rotten honey" (p. 200) that is their alcohol. Irresistible as honey, it is also rotten, poison that burns the mouth and transforms Lok and Fa into imitators of the given, so that the drunken Lok can proudly make the horrible admission: "I am one of the new people" (p. 202).

That we are, each of us, one of the new people is an unpleasant truth which we cannot evade. We are confronted with a view of human nature, profoundly pessimistic, as was the case in the *Lord of the Flies* too. Once again we are shown the Yahoo in us. We are made to see ourselves through the human nature for the first time. Seeing ourselves suddenly from the outside, we are astonished at our wickedness; made aware of the life of civilized man to be the most pernicious race of little odious vermin that nature ever suffered to crawl upon the surface of the earth.[27] In the *Lord of the Flies* we are taken to a remote island peopled by little men, whose behaviour represents in miniature our own foibles and failings, our folly and outright viciousness.

We habitually think of ourselves as the pinnacle and triumph of nature, "life's pride and cared-for crown," but to the eye of the disinterested outsider we appear to be an affront to nature, our nature verminous and parasitic, our success that of a particularly virulent disease. Nature would be ashamed at us, would disown us: Fa speaks for Oa, we may be sure, with the remarks of the new people: "Oa did not bring them out of her belly" (p. 173). Seeing ourselves through the eyes of innocence has the effect of making us ashamed of our humanity.

Such shame is perhaps the most abiding impression we take from *The Inheritors* and its outline of the angst-ridden psychology necessary in the struggle for survival makes it a deeply pessimistic work. However, Kinkead Weekes and Gregor have very clearly shown, the thrust of the novel is not simply to lament the disappearance of all things good and admirable in the shape of Lok's people and deplore the unqualified catastrophe of our arrival and rise to power. It seems to Lok that the new people are like fire, but they also seem to him like honey.

Their triumph involves much destruction and is qualified by the fear and grief which grip them mercilessly, but out of it may come a sweetness. One good which will arise from their costly advance in the creation of great art, a human contribution to the world which Oa's teeming belly could never produce. Our fallen nature leads to many misfortune and enormities but it also makes the creation of art possible which has the depth and emotional power of tragedy. The consciousness of people may seem to us eminently poetic but they themselves are no poets and the poetry in which Golding clothes them is limited to marvelous description of nature and gains much of its power by contrast with our own fallen vision.

Lok is left to die with only the little Oa for company. This is an image of the nature-mother and is itself a natural object. It is not an artifact, not a work of evil: Lok merely found it lying around, he did not shape or change it. For change, for creativity we must look at the new people.

Tuami is their artist and at the close he is meditating on the shape he will create. His art cuts into the marble, is creative, exploratory as great art is. It also grows out of the violent, quarrelsome, fallen nature of the new people. It is their nature of explore.

The potential of the new people for the creation of great and tragic art is perhaps one chink of light in the general gloom. Another cause of cautious optimism is the adoption into the new people of the "new one," the infant survivor of Lok's people. Perhaps one day there will be an inter-breeding between the new people and the last Neanderthals. Perhaps something of the goodness and gentleness will thus be introduced into human kind and then we would be the inheritors of that race too. After all, the experience of reading the novel shows that we can feel sympathy for the alien Neanderthals and we are also capable of shame at the excesses of our own kind. Without meeting with the new people, we uncover all the troubles and miseries in the world, but at the last there is still a token of hope.

NOTES

1. J.S. Ryan, "The Two Pincher Martins: From Survival Adventure to Golding's Myth of Dying," *English Studies*, 55 (1974), p. 142.
2. Frank Kermode, *Modern Essays* (London: Fountana Books, 1971), p. 240.
3. William Golding, "Digging for Pictures," *The Hot Gates and Other Occasional Pieces* (London: Faber and Faber), p. 69.
4. *Ibid.*, p. 70.
5. Rexroth, op. cit., p. 98.
6. As quoted in the epigraph to the novel, William Golding, *The Inheritors* (London: Faber and Faber), 1955.
7. Douglas M. Davis, "A Conversation with Golding," *New Republic*, CKV VII (4 May 1963), p. 30.
8. "The Writer in his Age," A reply to a questionnaire, *London Magazine* (10 May 1957), p. 46.
9. Kenneth Rexroth, "William Golding," CCXV, *Atlantic*, 21 (May, 1965), p. 98.
10. Louis J. Walle, *Out of Chaos* (Boston: Houghton Mufflin Company, 1977), p. 241.
11. Virginia Tiger, *William Golding: The Dark Fields of Discovery* (London: Calder & Boyars, 1974), p. 72.

12. Rexroth, op. cit., p. 98.
13. As quoted by Bernard S. Oldsey and Stanley Weinthraub, *The Art of William Golding* (New York: Harcourt, Brace and World, Inc., 1965), p. 72.
14. Rexroth, op. cit., p. 98.
15. Remarks attributed to Mr. Golding are derived from a transcript of a BBC discussion programme—interviewed by Prof. Kermode; Third programme (28 August 1959), and published in *Books and Bookmen*, V (Oct. 1959), pp. 9-10.
16. *Ibid.*
17. Frank Kermode, "Coral Islands," *Spectator* (22 Aug. 1958), p. 257.
18. Wordsworth, *Poetical Works*, p. 164 (*Tintern Abbey*, 1.49) Coleridge, *Poetical Works*, p. 101 (*The Eolian Harp*, 1.26).
19. He quoted the writer of the second Esdra: "A grain of evil was sown in the heart of Adam from the beginning...." *Myth & Guilt: The Crime & Punishment of Mankind* (New York Brazillea Inc.), p. 328.
20. Gabriel Josipovici, *The World and the Book: A Study of Modern Fiction* (Stanford: Stanford University Press, London, 1971), pp. 242-43.
21. *Ibid.*
22. William Golding, *Free Fall* (London: Faber and Faber, 1959), p. 78.
23. Josipovici, pp. 240-41.
24. As quoted by Erich Fromm, op. cit., pp. 229-30.
25. James Gindin, "Gimmick and Metaphor in the Novels of William Golding," *Modern Fiction Studies*, 6 (Summer 1960), p. 148.
26. Samuel Hynes, *William Golding* (New York: Columbia University Press, 1968), p. 23.
27. Swift, *Gulliver's Travels*, p. 107 (Bk. II, Ch. 6).

Conclusion

4

We live in an age of material prosperity and spiritual atrophy. Scientific knowledge breaks barriers everyday to bring within its realms new amazing vistas. In wide-mouthed wonder, man looks at these new ever-expanding avenues of knowledge to ignore the need for stability sustained by moral values. The twentieth-century intellectual is a spiritual drifter. He lacks a sense of direction and purpose. We need writers who can, in no uncertain terms, describe the malady, if not suggest the remedial measures. The answer to the problem has been offered by writers like Evelyn Waugh, Graham Greene, Iris Murdoch and William Golding.

The understanding of the world shown by these contemporary novelists includes assessments of the nature of good and evil and of the 'immanence of God' perhaps encouraged by the imminence of actuality of war. Good and evil can be considered extension of the 'halves' of peace and violence, innocence and experience, which Newby envisaged as the result of the war's impact on contemporary life. The circumstances of the war furthered belief and interest in the existence of 'a real something called Evil.' Britain's struggle against Fascism and Nazi Germany was very frequently seen at the time and with some conviction, as a struggle against evil and the powers of darkness. Stephen Spender,[1] remarks in *Penguin New Writing* in 1941 that 'The angels and the demons of an earlier time, have simply been suppressed in our consciousness that is all,' and he adds emphatically that Fascism is "a deliberately chosen life of damnation...macabre, diabolism"[2] Cyril Connolly suggests that Nazism was simply an "opposite" to "goodness and sanity."[3] This sense of conflict between madness and sanity, good and evil appears in Golding's works.

His religious concerns are also brought to the foreground by the war. Golding has commented in several places that before World War II, he trusted in the efficacy of social and political effort. Afterwards he profoundly distrusted man's potential for progress. Not that the basic nature of man has changed in three decades since the bomb, for as he remarks "surely the hydrogen bomb is only an efficient way of wiping out the other tribe—a pastime we've always been prone to."[4] The war witnessed again man's inhumanity to man. Golding remarked "I started to write late and I have reached certain conclusions. I have always been struck by the things which men do to other men. I know of deeds which took place during the war, about which I still cannot think without feeling physically ill."[5]

A direct consequence of this sort of pessimistic Aeschylean preoccupation with the human tragedy[6] where his novels, which question a whole tradition embodying man's simplistic and optimistic formulations about himself. His work, mainly based on his own painful observation of the cult of the irrational and on his non war-time experiences, seems a counter-blast to the eighteenth-century rationalists Herder, Kant, and Schiller, the nineteenth-century biologists like James G. Frazer and Edward B. Taylor and such liberal thinkers in modern times as H.G. Wells and Sir Julian Huxley.

Many writers have been concerned with what is rhetorically called "the dilemma of modern man" and have given us lantern slide pictures on the anarchy of a poisoned future. Their really essayists sitting in comfort.

Sartre has offered novels and plays in which existentialism is conveyed not as a set of concepts, but as experience. Few professional theologians have tried to do for Christianity what Sartre has done for existentialism, yet the theologians who have spoken most compellingly in the last two generations have been men who in Tillich's phrase, have sought to "correlate theological answers with existential questions"[7]—who have understood the theological task not as the preservation and handling on of an orthodox tradition, but as a way of engaging with the dynamics of existence so as to clarify in the light of Christian faith the fullest range of human experience and consciousness. In this endeavour, the theological value of the exploration of the human plight in contemporary art and literature has been recognized. Tillich's indebtedness is well known and the work of Golding has attracted the interest of theologians.

Golding came to tackle the moral wretchedness which he saw in the fragmented society and man of the twentieth-century who are so inured to depravity.

Golding's books are novels, with all the density, ambiguity and concreteness of an art-form, far removed, it would seem, from the systemized abstractions suggested by theology. Yet as Dennis Keene has said:

> the novels do not make sense unless one remembers that Golding is a Christian writer. His novels are not theology in the academic sense, but it can hardly be disputed that they are theologically oriented.[8]

Samuel Hynes notes that Golding's works are the "Novels of a Religious Man,"[9] and Juliet Mitchell claims that they are ostensibly based on Christian theology and use inversions and paradoxes based on Christian themes to impart an impression of philosophical discovery.[10]

The preoccupations are widely religious ones—he treats such perennial themes as innocence, guilt, mystery and malignancy quite purposefully in their antique religious sense. He consciously tries to construct a religious mythopoeia relevant to contemporary man. In Golding's view contemporary man lacks vision, he discounts the spiritual world, but it in Golding's view does not discount him. Thus contemporary man experiences mystery as a dark thing.

The theology implied by Golding's novels is in some respects rather old fashioned. The novels invite us to experience humanness in terms of man's relationship to transcendent being and to consider the demonic distortion of humanness which results when that relationship is ruptured. Golding's God thus appears as an authoritarian deity who demands surrender and obedience and negates human titanism. This is not popular theology today, when there is an emphasis on man's having come of age and God tends to be reduced to a mere inspirer and endorser of secular programmes. Today, the tendency is to discard everything in traditional Christianity which cannot be accommodated to prevailing secular values. This theology starts from a positivistic funding of all reality into the mundane and eliminates the doctrine of God's otherness, claiming to discover divinity in the highest human values and to leave room for human responsibility and freedom. There is insight in such theology, it defines a pole of theological truth which has needed new recognition and reorientation. But it tends to become an inoffensive creed hardly worth an agnostics disagreement. The opposite pole of theological truth is obscured, and one of the first things to go is the biblical doctrine of the wrath of God. The traditional picture of hell may be morally repugnant; yet rejection of that picture need not leave us with a God whose concern for righteousness is minimal and whose love is only the affirmation of man as he now is. Golding creates a kind of extreme experience in which the wrath of God becomes existentially significant as a disruption of man's version of reality and a negation of the distorted ego which invents it.

Golding once said that he had no solutions "ever" but he forces us into extreme forms of experience which give rise to a number of disturbing paradoxes. Human consciousness seems to be split between opposing modes of reality; essence and existence, innocence and guilt, the absolute and the relative, the divine and the demonic, the self and the other. No conceptual scheme can harmonize the contraries. All systematization of experience are reductionist in that they fail to encompass the full distance between the poles of consciousness. There is no bridge between the two worlds, but both worlds are equally real.

However, the consciousness of the split must imply some residual awareness of a unitary reality, some knowledge of a prelapsarian state in which there was a single, unfractured vision. Such vision perhaps belong to childhood, but in *The Inheritors* Golding locates it in an archetypal innocence he describes in mythological form. His Neanderthal is man before Adam's Fall. Golding does not merely describe Neanderthalers from the outside as an anthropologist would do; he attempts to enter their consciousness, to experience existence as they experience it. We respond to his skill by recognizing the recess in our own being where we remember that reality was once unfractured, and our minds fill with echoes of primal innocence and lost Edens.

The doctrine of Golding stands by virtue of its explanatory power and not in orthodoxy and the experiences enacted and communicated by Golding are the kind of experiences in which the Christian doctrine of man becomes existentially significant in terms of explanatory power. In his novels the absence of God from the center of human consciousness is explored. Such absence can take two forms. In one, God as absent simply because He is unnecessary. The only meanings are those which man himself creates and the puzzles and predicaments of existence are solved by human rationality scientifically applied. This view is represented by Piggy (*Lord of the Flies*).

But with another form of the absence of God the rationalism of Piggy and Pincher is powerless to deal. The true God is absent, but his place has been taken by a distorted, demonic image. Golding enacts experiences which reveals that the rationalist hope is based upon a reductionist account of human awareness. Man is haunted by the supernatural, by a reality that transcends his own power of mastery and order and presents itself as a rival contender in the power games, requiring some kind of propitiation. The boys on the island and the 'new people' in *The Inheritors* are afraid of devils; Pincher Martin is overwhelmed by "the black lightning." The consequences are murder, cannibalism, madness, despair.

It is possible to argue as Piggy does, that demons do not exist and that a cool rationalism will expose the deception. The impotence of this programme is, Golding shows, due to the fact that man comes to cherish the demons, because they endorse his own will to power. The demons are objectifications of lust masquerading as ultimate reality and man needs the demons because they are the means by which he writes himself large upon the Universe. He may address the demons as God and claim that his own hubris is service of the divine will. The demons *do* exist, but they exist as terrible perversions of transcendental reality.

As a writer of intense visual gift, an overpowering sense of nature, an extraordinary perception of man as a physical being in a physical world, torn between a primitive inheritance and the glimmer of an evolving mind and as a writer familiar with the strong emotions that go with the instinct for self-preservation, blind love for his kind, hatred, fear and elation, he has been able to shake us until we feel in our bones the perennial agony of our species.

Pain is the essence of his subject. And there's pity for their pain. In *The Inheritors* it is the obscure pain of a baffled and dying group of ape-man who see themselves supplanted by the more skilful new being called man. The ape-man experiences the pain of the grunt, of trying to communicate from one poor mind to another—"I have a picture. Can you see my picture"—and also the pain of trying to distinguish what is inside from what is outside himself. He sees with a kind of grieving as an animal might grieve. In *Pincher Martin* the tale of a modern sailor whose broken body is washed about the Atlantic rock, who eats limpets, is poisoned by his store of food and who eventually goes mad and dies, the pain is in the fight against physical hurt and loss of consciousness, in the struggle to put his educated will against his terrors. It is also in the Job-like protest against a defeat which wrongs everything he believed in. In *Lord of the Flies* the pain is in the struggle between the boys, who revert, through fear, to the primitive and turn into savage hunters and those who are trying vainly to preserve foresight and order. In the end, the boys are rescued but not before they have lived through the modern political nightmare.

From the beginning, he has written under the influence of dominant ideas rather than dominant people, for he explained that both upbringing and nature kept him from an immediate delight in people. This retirement from the battle of personal and social life has left him free to explore a lifelong pre-occupation with the nature of the Universe.

His work demonstrates the limitations of order envisaged by the rational consciousness of man. Man dreams of a rational, well structured Universe, but Golding suggests that the Universal order defies all rational efforts to fully grasp its complexity, to resolve its seeming contradictions and to reconcile its incompatible and disparate elements.

He visualizes the Universe as "cosmic chaos." In an interview with Owen Webster he has remarked that the basic problem of modern man "is learning to live fearlessly with the natural chaos of existence, without forcing artificial patterns on it."[11] Yet, at the same time there is the nagging awareness that it can never represent the actual reality. The dilemma facing those who quest for order and pattern may be expressed in words of Karen Henz in J.C. Oates's work: it is "insane to look for meaning in life and it is insane not to."[12] Indeed, "the challenge of composing order, constitutes the very essence of the human situation."[13]

His fiction focuses on this significant aspect of man questing for order on various levels and encountering in the process chaos within and without. Chaos, in Golding's world manifests itself in various forms. On the social level it is seen in the form of violence resulting from the clash between different types of order (*Lord of the Flies*). It is also experienced in the form of moral evil and seen as resulting from over-assertion of the ego (*Pincher Martin*).

Another variant of this is "the darkness of man's heart" glimpsed by Ralph (*Lord of the Flies*) and Pincher Martin. They experience in the end a sense of their own "complicity with evil."[14] Again, there is the fallen man's sense of chaos, his sense of separateness or alienation from the Universe.

Golding visualizes a state in which man lived in perfect harmony with the Universe (*The Inheritors*). Man was a perfect microcosm of the macrocosm. Being unself-conscious, he was never aware of nature as other, and was absolutely free of the tension between order and chaos. Golding depicts man's loss of the sense of unity with the Universe with the fragmentation of his undifferentiated consciousness. Man's rise to consciousness is seen by Golding as a Fall. Man is destined to endure the trials of self, ranging from an adolescent's awareness of the ignominy of growing up through the deceptive and self-deceptive subterfuges of a noble aspiration to the seriocomic rites of passage, to an adult sense of sin and selfhood, disgrace and defilement and ignominy and guilt. In Golding's Universe the descent of man is enacted not in the Darwinian sense, but literally and in the theological sense of the Fall. While the doctrinal Fall forms the skeletal background, Golding depicts the Fall not as occurring in the history of the human species (*The Inheritors*), but as a destined event, in the Blakean sense, in the life of social class (*Lord of the Flies*) or in that of every individual (*Pincher Martin*) as he moves from Innocence to Experience.

His novels are parables of caution and reflect his view that "The arbitrary checks...are nothing but...the bitter experiences of people who are adult enough to realize, 'well I, I myself am vicious and would like to kill that man, and he is vicious and would like to kill me.'"[15] The horror of existence without these arbitrary checks is the most consistent theme in Golding. He is convinced that when man denies those checks that insure him freedom (his only ennoblement in an absurd universe), his existence is contemptible. He is convinced that without the restraint of social order, human being will "sink below the level of the beast."[16] This is Golding's major statement, and a consistent and existential point of view emerges when we pierce beyond the idiosyncrasies of his style.

Men do terrible things when they act in the name of religion and claim divine authority of their programmes. Precisely because it points to a transcendent reality, religion can tempt a man into the belief that he can himself attain transcendence, that he can climb out of the relativism and finitude of his condition and attain absolute truth. Here, we find the deepest paradoxes of human consciousness that man touches the fringe of the eternal, that he glimpses the infinite, and yet knows himself to be subject to temporality. So it is that he build towers of Babel from which to survey his condition and claim equality with God. But the towers are never high enough. Like the original tower, they are unfinished, witnessing to the inevitable limitations of human endeavour and to the hubris which has attempted to go beyond them. Human pride is one aspect of what Christian orthodoxy means by Original sin. The importance of this doctrine lies in its recognition of evil in the best of human actions. We do not require a doctrine to remind us of man's violence and barbarism, what we need is a doctrine that questions his noblest dreams and his most sublime inventions. Only man's recognition of his fallenness, of the distance that separates him from God, can safeguard him from the attribution of absolute authority of his programmes. Golding has shown what happens when a man forgets his fallenness. Man's vision is tainted by motives springing from self-regard. The effect is to unleash destructive forces that bring about unthinkable disaster.

He deals with man's instinct to destroy what is good, whether it is material or spiritual. Treating of cruelty, selfishness and yearning after power, he puts his viewpoint very clearly, evil is apparent everywhere and is with difficulty held at bay, and good is almost impossible to achieve.

Lord of the Flies and *The Inheritors* show something of the origin of evil within the species, its inherent presence within 'civilized' man (which he has inherited from Adam) and its inevitable connection with individual will. Set in contexts remote in time and space from everyday life, each is essentially a fable, illustrative of a particular fact of the truth about man and his nature. As John Wain pointed out in 1962:

> William Golding...is not a novelist...he is an allegorist. He has certain perceptions about the human condition which he...goes ahead and creates an allegory to represent.[17]

Depressing truths about "man and his nature" are presented throughout his works.

Lord of the Flies with its island setting isolated from the complexities of society, the exclusiveness of its characters, not merely children but boys before puberty, the firm direction of its plot; all minister to the creation of a deliberate artifact which is the hallmark of a fable.

But there is an important openness in the presentation, especially of Piggy and Simon, which raises questions about the overt design of the book, giving it a new dimension of interest. This dimension is the stirring of myth imagination in a world primarily fabulous. Golding's imagination is more complex and less articulate than his design and structure. His basic art is one of revelation than demonstration and what is eventually revealed is more mysterious than what the author or reader expected.

Lord of the Flies demonstrates what the novel defines as "the end of innocence, the darkness of man's heart."[18] Golding develops this theme in loose analogy with the Bible story of Original sin in the Garden of Eden. This novel traces the degeneration and the innate brutality of a group of boys abandoned on a paradisiacal desert island from civilization into barbarism and an allegiance to the Lord of the flies—a name for the devil.

He emphasizes that the children, vulnerable and ignorant of their own nature can do the most terrible things. Their ignorance is confused with innocence, Golding firmly believes that the root of our sin is there, in the child. As soon as it has any capacity for acting on the world outside, it will be selfish; and of course, Original sin and Selfishness are interchangeable. You can only learn unselfishness through liking and loving. And children's love can be absolute, passionate and profound. And this is where their unselfishness comes, through their need of love; so that anything they can do for this demigod, is something their happy to do.

When Ralph cries, at the end for "the darkness of man's heart" (p. 248), he weeps for the forces of violence in the island whose triumph has been averted only by the chance arrival of a ship. Simon, alone among the boys, acts with the intuitive belief that some rescue may be possible. In his encounter with the emblem of violence and fear, the Head on the stick, there is the first appearance of the theme which the later fable elaborate and extend. Man, in fear, abstracts from his own brutality, and projects it as a demon or ogre which will destroy him.

The Inheritors is a long leap forward. In one sense, at the level of 'subject' Golding takes a world so completely 'other' that it seems unequivocally to invite the description of fable, taking its place with Utopia, Brobdingnag, Erewhon. Moreover, he seems to have begun from a thesis-quarrel, a conscious design to demonstrate the inadequacies of Wells. But Golding establishes the novel's "otherworld" by employing all his imaginative resources not as More, Swift and Butler do, to manoeuvre analytically between 'their' world and 'ours' but rather to make us forget our world and become imaginatively immersed in the dense mystery of his. The essential element in it is the discovery of a procedure which inhibits analysis and judgment, becoming for the first time essentially explorative and tentative. In other words, the datum of *The Inheritors* seems to belong to fable, but its whole realization belongs to history in which myth is located by imaginative exploration. *The Inheritors* locates this psychic and moral evasion in prehistoric times and uses it to account for the genesis of guilt in man. This novel also examines "the end of innocence, the darkness of man's heart, but on a still larger, more nearly mythic scale. The innocence lost is of Neanderthal man, eradicated in prehistory by the darkness at the heart of *Homosapiens*, a new species endowed with possession, skill and malice, a people of the Fall. Its members are intelligent, equipped with reason and art, but their simultaneous capacity for hatred, crime and superstition alienates them from nature and even from each other, making them a sad alternative to their predecessors."[19]

The New People project their terror and uncertainty upon the Neanderthals and in doing so impart to the prelapsarians their own aggressive, rapacious nature. Thus when Tuami broods upon 'the line of darkness' (p. 233) at the end, he is brooding upon his own internal landscape, his own guilty darkness.

In *The Inheritors* Golding tried to reveal the nature of man by imagining his origins. We are manipulated into a position of complicity with guilt, through uncomprehending eyes. This knowledge does not flatter us, it condemns us. Although we are inclined to sympathise with Lok's people, Golding's technique forces us to realize that we belong with the New Man, we are the 'Inheritors.' The novel calls into question precisely what it is we have inherited and suggests that principal among our legacies is guilt.

This is an issue which is central to *Pincher Martin* as well. From the beginning, the New Men, are associated with disruption, violence and death. The title seems to contain a sombre pun on "Blessed are the meek for they shall inherit the earth" (Mathew, 5:5), as throughout the course of this novel, we realize that here the meek do not 'inherit' the earth, rather we, *Homosapiens* do—and the meek are completely destroyed.

The *Pincher Martin* marks an end and a beginning: the end of a set of novels in which the state of man is explored as a finite concept; the beginning of a set, in which complex, searching, philosophically difficult questions begin to be asked about how one should look at man. These are necessarily more difficult, obscure and tortured for both author and reader, for they are about authorship and ways of reading. The protagonist becomes himself an artist asking not just "what am I?," but also "how did I become what I am," and "how do I find a way of looking at my being and becoming that will reconcile the contradictions I see?".

Golding's excellence as a novelist is the gift of graphic imagination which enables him not just to allege but to characterize the dire limitations of optimism, scientific rationalism and any facile concept of "progress." His novels take a radical view of the human condition and emphasise its evil, egotism and guilt. His artistic vision is essentially spiritual. He remarks: "I'm, in fact, an Ancient Egyptian, with all their unreason, spiritual pragmatism and capacity for ambiguous belief."[20]

His fictions are less didactic declarations than painfully imagined demonstrations of the chaos human nature has brought upon itself, less solutions than felt responses. Golding credits the sanctions of a civilized society and he intimates the reality of saintliness on sanctity, the possibility of grace and redemption. "I don't like to be thought of a person which says man is beastly." He has said "I'm really an optimist. Simon is the whole point of *Lord of the Flies* and Simon is love."[21] In answer to readers who may believe that he insists upon one negative 'moral'—that mankind exhibits nothing but self-engendered corruption, Golding has responded that the only kind of progress is the progress of the individual towards some kind of an *ethical* integration and his consequent effect upon people who are near him.

His prime concern as a novelist has been to make us aware of areas of existence behind or beyond man's rational being in the universe. These areas may be the metaphysical realm, the spirit world, man's inner nature, the visionary, or man's intellectual life in uneasy balance with his historic past. In his daily life in the world of work and relationship man is blind or oblivious to these areas. Golding's novels make us see them, make us aware of their presence in the universe we inhabit.

It is through words organized into structure that Golding makes us see relations of experience and being that are beyond the limits of language. It is these linguistic structures which reveal more than language can describe that are the subject of his book.

The writer lives now in a world which has ceased to be explicit because it has ceased to be explicable. Golding indicates that the goal of his art is to make the reader see the universe in all its complexity. "In all my works I have suggested a shape in the Universe that may, as it were, account for things."[22] But Golding's 'account' of things does not consist of putting forward an explanation for the action described in the novels. In fact there are no explanations at all. The reader is shown or made aware of complexity, mystery and areas of existence that escape rational analysis. Golding's art is an art of discovery. The discovery it makes is that the universe is inexplicable and cannot be wholly described in words and yet words are all that the novelist has with which to describe the universe. The problem of language and its relationship to physical and metaphysical worlds is a theme Golding continually returns to. In fact, we could say that it is what his art is about. Through words alone, he can make us aware of areas of existence which are beyond the limits of language. This is one of the great strengths of his writing. *Pincher Martin* describes Martin's suffering at the same time makes us realise that the physical battle is in reality a metaphysical struggle, with the use of our everyday language. The breakdown in communication between Campbell and Davidson occurs because Campbell asks a question beyond everyday existence in ordinary language. Davidson accepts the ordinariness and misses the point of the question. However, by the end of the novel we understand Campbell's question and realize Davidson has misunderstood it.

In all his novels, Golding has been concerned with man's fallen nature and with the relation of the Fall to the blighting self-consciousness of which language is a product. Language is a sign of loss of innocence and of the longing for redemption to which the loss gives rise. Religious tradition, in which speech is associated with the Fall, gives his attitude authority. Genesis first mentions speech in the Temptation—We find that Eve a woman spoke before all others, in answer to the enquiry of the devil.

The Inheritors centred upon the unfallen world, is most explicity concerned with language and guilt. Eleven of its twelve chapters describes the prearticulate condition of the predecessors of *Homosapiens*. They are unfallen and possess a happiness their inheritors can never enjoy. Their Angelic conversations were intuitive and did not need words as human discourse did. Lok's people, just beyond the evolutionary bar, are not entirely without language or reason, they have a little of both, but rely upon neither. To the new people, they are animal, partly because they cannot really talk, partly because they exhibit an animal's immersion in sensual experience. Yet that total reliance upon the senses, which makes Lok's people brutes, implies an attitude towards life which is the antithesis of brutality. It is Tuami's people not Lok's, who are bestial. Because they respond to immediate demands of the senses, Lok's people inhabit a world free from notions of past and future and innocent of apprehension or possession. They search for food and fuel collaboratively in response to hunger and cold, and they seek to satisfy no more than those needs. Provision for more than the morrow characteristic of his successors, baffles primitive Lok.

Only in *The Inheritors* does Golding present the experience of innocence as a prelapsarian condition. Yet the innocent can be found elsewhere, amongst those who, though subject to a cosmic fall, have not succumbed to a personal one. This is not a prerogative of childhood. The adult may retain his innocence as Nat in *Pincher Martin* whilst the child may already be fallen like, Jack in *Lord of the Flies*.

The fallen of Golding's novels particularly Pincher, have more to do with the contemporary world than do his innocents, for the fallen seem to represent what civilization has become. Pincher undergoes the miseries of a consciousness abandoned to the pitiful spiritual resources of that civilization on which his innocent friend Nat is an oblique comment, as an image both of what it abuses and what it has lost. Where Nat's language is sparing in both senses, Pincher shows its profit as being knowing how to curse. Nevertheless, he regards language as redemptive. Golding often has recourse to the language of religion as the novels deal with vision. It was for him the noble instrument of man's conversation with God.

The questions that preoccupy Golding relate finally to the process of artistic creation, and creativity may prove redemptive and furnish a return to innocence. All central figures of the novels are in a sense artists—Jack and Simon are Choristers, Tuami a carver and Pincher Martin an actor. They are artists because the creative imagination is most deeply responsive and the torment of the Fall and its aspirations to perfection are consequently the most intense. The artist is the guiltiest of human beings for the range of his insights and emotions is the most comprehensive. *Pincher Martin* considers the relation of human guilt, language, and art, as it is written from a conviction that art is the monument to man's Fall. Pincher's experience of the rocks makes this explicit, since the narrative as the ending reveals, has no existence outside the mind. The refusal of the brain to accept annihilation has created the geography and history of its purgatorial torment, and the prose of the novel is a sustained mimesis of the effort that sustains such a fiction.

In order to bring about the reader's imaginative participation in the events and insights of his fables, he has devised numerous fictional techniques based for the most part on technical compression. He constructs rigorous structures and exclusive forms to illustrate his own inconclusive vision.

Basically Golding's novels grow through the tension between its form and his imagination. This tension can be described by bringing together forms 'fable,' 'history' and 'myth.' They are three different ways of looking at life, each of which has a different stance towards "truth." Each has a fundamental strength of a different sort, but when looked at from an angle other than its own, each has also fundamental limitations. From the viewpoint of history, myth and fable seem too rigidly patterned taking too exclusive a grip on the complex processes of life. From the view of fable, history is a baggy monster, capable of testifying only to its own muddle; while myth is mystification, depriving itself of intellectual freedom through its pretensions to a historical reality. From the view point of myth, history tries to include too much, fable too little.

Each mode affords a definably different satisfaction as it proceeds from a diverse imaginative urge. Fable offers the pleasures of analysis, history those of recognition, myth these of revelation. To see the varying treatments of characters in these different modes is to see from another angle their distinctive emphasis. Myth like history, persuades us that its characters are real people in real places, but it has links with fable in that it persuades us to question the nature of this reality. Unlike fable, however, the revelation of myth is gradual, unobtrusive, taking shape beneath the surface. As far as presentation of character is concerned, this means that individual features fade to reveal archetypal forces.

His mode is not history but myth, in that it seeks to reveal archetypal truth within history. In *Lord of the Flies* we are continually made to look at a scene in order to pinpoint its significance within the whole analysis; in *The Inheritors* we are drawn into the scene, incapable of seeing where we are going, but immersed in a mysterious act of discovery.

Golding's text includes obscurity as a large element in its plot. Obscurity is either deliberate or inevitable. 'Obscure' implies that behind the opaqueness of the texts there is a clarity, a truth, which the author is trying to make us see, but which is almost impossible to describe in plain language. Golding attempts to make us aware of regions of experience, of the presence of mystery, darkness and the unknown areas that lie beneath the surface of everyday being. It is precisely because they are below the surface of ordinary life and beyond the common linguistic currency with which we describe our relationship to the universe that Golding's methods in making us see these truths which are indirect and obscure.

James R. Baker remarked to Golding that "in an aesthetic age you have been one who insists upon mystery, on the neglected or perhaps forgotten religious dimensions of human experience." Has this been a deliberate course on your part, a sort of counteraction or corrective to our diminished sense of the numinous? To which Golding replied:

> I'd like to think it was a corrective to what you call a diminished sense of the numinous. Whether it is or not, whether that kind of Holy-Joeing may not simply just put people off, I don't know. But it seems natural to me.[23]

Our reaction makes us aware of our own consciousness and we begin to map out our awareness of ourselves. A major feature of his novels is this centripetal quality, their inward concentration on the worlds they map out. The novels are mirrors in which we view, the interior of our being.

In an essay on Baudelaire, the German critic, Walter Benjamin said that "The person we look at, or who feels he is being looked at, looks at us in turn. To perceive the aura of an object we look at means to invest it with the ability to look at us in turn."[24] Golding's novels are such objects.

Deriving from Golding's concern with the spiritual and contemporary man's apparent rejection of this reaction is the unorthodox structure of each of the novels. Virginia Tiger remarks that although the novels of Golding do not openly explain events in religious terms, they demand from the reader a religious interpretation. He creates an ideographic structure in each of these fables to allow two contradictory perspectives on one circumstance.

Tiger adopts the conception that the reader creates as he or she reads and links this to the structure of the novels, which she calls 'ideographic.'

> The ideographic structure seems, at first reading, to create two contradicting perspectives on the same circumstances since the idea reverses the expectations which the first movement has built up...the two perspectives can be linked together by the reader.... In forcing the reader to build the bridge between contradictory perspectives, the ideographic structure forces the reader to...encounter, by the imaginative impact of words, those experiences which conventionally words do not reach...the primacy of spiritual experience itself. The ideographic structure grows from his belief that "where there is no vision the people perish."[25]

Following the plot's major development there is a coda ending in each of the fables which reverses and often contradicts the implications of the first movement. But Golding intends the two perspectives to be linked, not contradictory and thereby force an awareness of the spiritual dimension, since this is the explanation that will provide the link between the two. The bridge between the two perspectives is to be built by the reader who is driven by the paradoxical structure of the novel to accept paradoxes of existence which are to Golding symptoms of the spiritual world.

The final chapter focuses attention on the impressions made by Golding's novels; to see the particular kind of 'will' that Golding has exerted over us. It appears as something heavily patterned, uniformly intense and severely exclusive. The patterning can be observed even in the externalities of length and chapter division, which is virtually the same in every novel. The general form is markedly dialectical that we are led into describing each novel in terms of different worlds brought into stark confrontation. The moment of confrontation is of high dramatic intensity. The books are uniformly intense in that the mood in which each is written hardly changes; though there are shifts in the point of view. The central characters interrogate themselves remorselessly, alter, but always they remain the eye of a storm. Related to this homogeneity of mood is the dominant impression of exclusiveness. The shaping spirit of the imagination seems always at work in the foreground of our attention. However densely imagined a particular character or episode may be, everything has been stripped of irrelevant detail. Bringing these impressions together we can conclude that a Golding novel gives the effect of something dedicately made.

At the heart of each fable Golding constructs a psychic and purgative episode where a reductive process is enacted to bring the character up against this world. He presents character in *extremis* not only through torment but in torment. In this process the protagonist is stripped down to that very last thing which cannot be destroyed; this Golding takes as a definition of the particular Being. In the confrontation scene which precedes such atavistic reductions the character is forced to accept or reject the darkness that inhabits his internal landscape.

In *Lord of the Flies* and *Pincher Martin* this encounter takes the form of an interview with an ambiguous but obscurely animated object: a Pig's Head, and a pile of stones, respectively. Following his conversation with the Head, Simon falls inside its vast mouth and the 'blackness within, a blackness that spread' (p. 178). On regaining consciousness, he is able to recognize himself in the Head and having admitted evil is able to act without evil.

Thus in *Lord of the Flies*, just as the children assume demonic proportions in their regression, there is a coda ending where they are cut down to child-size since they are viewed by an adult. But there is the further paradox that the officer who rescues the children is himself involved in an "adult war, a good deal more potentially violent and widespread than that of the children. Therefore, the compassion Ralph achieves represents a hard-won knowledge which the officer himself does not possess.

In *The Inheritors* there are two perspectives on the same events, that of the innocent Neanderthals and that of the inheritors themselves, the violent New People who demonstrate in their efficient skill that the meek do not inherit the earth. Yet neither do the violent, nor the New People have been irrevocably altered by their fear in the tree-orgies, guilt and introspection have been evolved.

The confrontation scene in *The Inheritors* occurs when a nightmare specter emerges in the world of water as Lok leans out across the river, suspended from a tree branch. Though it is a reflection of his own face, symbolically the Lok-face represents a formless thing, a terrifying stranger disengaged and alienated from his own psyche. When the body of the old woman descends the river and drifts past him, the two specters merge and it becomes clear that what is being dramatized here is the opposition of the two worlds of innocence and guilt.

Golding uses the structure of the novels, their form and organization, as the medium of meaning. The complexity of the novels forces the reader into the recreative act of restructuring the text, and in experiencing this he experiences mystery and paradox as he attempts to find an explanation for the events described. The structure forces us to find a perspective that will encompass all that has happened in the text. The fact that the reader is continually baulked makes him confront the nature of mystery of the unsayable, and therefore brings him face to face with the inexplicable nature of the universe. The novels can therefore be seen as more about the process of reading and perception than they are about boys on an island, about the *Homosapiens* and the New man, or about the sufferings of Christopher Hadley Martin.

The difference between the text and the world is emphasized —through remote settings, confined worlds, chronological shifts, restricted narrative point of view, changes in perspectives, unusual characters—so that we are made aware of the act of reading, and his active participation has the effect of creating a new perception in him.

Dealing with theology does not mean spinning abstract formulations of non-empirical reality out of one's head. However remote and academic the theologian may seem, Golding asserts that his discourse has been prompted by events and experiences judged to be of cosmic significance and giving access to the way things ultimately are. This process also operates in reverse, when the creative imagination reenacts in the form of myth, the unpredictable experience, presupposed by doctrinal formulation. It can also enact experience which brings theological statement under appraisal and challenges its assumptions. Events and new knowledge can cause a disorientation calling for new theological solution. But how far a basic doctrine can be qualified and reinterpreted while remaining the same doctrine is a particularly perplexing question today. To give a specific example, which brings us near the center of Golding's concern, we may ask whether the traditional Christian doctrine of Original sin is still the same doctrine when its basis in the story of the Fall is recognized as myth not history, and when Original sin is interpreted not as the result of a primal rebellious act, but as an inevitable concomitant of man's existential condition. The Christian doctrine of Original sin is about the rupture of man's relationship with God; it is not about the incompleteness of evolutionary development. One factor that makes Golding a Christian writer is his recognition of the difference between these two anthropologies and his siding with the theological rather than the biblical version, though he also recognizes that the terms in which the Christian doctrine becomes existentially significant today will require a reformulation of orthodoxy.

Golding's novels are a great deal more than anything one can say about them. Any attempt to draw out meanings is bound to simplify, to ignore richness and density, to fasten on this part of the content rather than that, to treat the novels as problems to be solved rather than experiences to be entered. Inevitably, too, one's response is affected by one's own interpretation of life and one tends to find what one expects. A world of art, like experience itself, exists at many levels of meaning and can be matched to a variety of conceptual frames. The Christian frame is more inclusive than its rivals though this is not to say that every image and event has a counterpart in Christian doctrine. His work operates in some respects as a critique of Christian understanding, discarding the supernatural dimension of traditional belief and offering a phenomenological version of reality. He gives us new ways of imaging Christian doctrine, mythological enactments which are also in an important sense the modern equivalents of the archetypal stories in Genesis. And what he reformulates is recognizably the mainstream of Christian tradition, not some reduction of it.

His main frame is Christian theology with all its ennobling features, at the same his concern is deeply embedded Christian tradition. Compromising with theology and tradition, Golding brings out inherent values in Christianity in a variegated spectrum of incidents and characters akin to biblical concept within the ambit of accepted values in life.

NOTES

1. Stephen Spender, *Books and the War* (V) and *Books and the War* (VII).
2. *Penguin New Writing*, 1941, Nos. 6 and 8, pp. 129-30.
3. Cyril Connolly, Editorial in *Horizon*, 1941, p. 6.
4. Golding, "The Writer in His Age," *The London Magazine* (May 1957), p. 45.
5. Golding, "The Condition of the Novel," *New Left Review* (January-February 1965), p. 34.
6. Golding, "The Writer in His Age," p. 45.
7. Paul Tillich, *Systematic Theology* (Chicago: University of Chicago Press, 1957), 2, 15.
8. Dennis Keene, *William Golding and Jehovah* (Kyoto, Japan: University of Kyoto Press, 1963), p. 1.
9. Sam Hynes, "Novels of a Religious Man" *Commonweal*, 18 (March 1960), pp. 673-75.
10. Juliet Mitchell, "Concepts and Techniques in William Golding," *New Left Review* (May-June 1962), pp. 63-71.
11. Golding's phrase in interview with Owen Webster quoted by James R. Baker, *William Golding: A Critical Study* (New York: St. Martin's Press, 1965), p. 57.
12. J.C. Oates, *With Shuddering Fall* (New York: Vanguard Press, 1964), p. 315.

13. Iredell Jenkins, "The Modern Distemper: The Failure of Purposiveness," in *The Concept of Order*, ed. Paul G. Kuntz (Seattle and London: University of Washington Press, 1968), p. 427.
14. Arthur Miller's phrase quoted by Rollo May, *Power & Innocence* (New York: W.W. Norton & Co., Inc., 1972), p. 49.
15. Frank Kermode, "The Meaning of it All," *Books and Bookmen, 5* (October 1959), p. 9.
16. James Keating, *Interview with William Golding* Casebook ed., p. 194.
17. Interview with Frank Kermode, "The House of Fiction" in Malcolm Bradbury ed., *The Novel Today* (London: Fontana, 1977), p. 130.
18. William Golding, *Lord of the Flies* (1954; Rpt. London: Faber and Faber, 1967), p. 223.
19. William Golding, *The Inheritors* (1955; Rpt. London: Faber and Faber, 1979), pp. 163, 194-95.
20. William Golding, *The Hot Gates* (London: Faber and Faber, 1965), p. 82.
21. *Evening Herald*, 11 February, '63.
22. Golding in an Interview with Owen Webster, "Living with Chaos", *Books & Art* (March 1958), p. 16.
23. James R. Baker, "An Interview with William Golding," *Twentieth-Century Literature*, 28, No. 2 (Summer 1982), p. 169.
24. Water Benjamin, "On Some Motifs in Baudelaire," *Illuminations*, ed. Hanna Arendt. Trans. H. John (London: Fontana, 1973), p. 190.
25. Virginia Tiger, *William Golding: The Dark Fields of Discovery* (London: Calder & Boyars, 1974), pp. 17-18.

Bibliography

PRIMARY SOURCES

Works by William Golding

Lord of the Flies. London: Faber and Faber, 1954.

The Inheritors. London: Faber and Faber, 1955.

Pincher Martin. London: Faber and Faber, 1956.

The Hot Gates and Other Occasional Pieces. London: Faber and Faber, 1966.

A Moving Target. London: Faber and Faber, 1982.

Articles by Golding

Contribution to "The Writer in His Age," *London Magazine*. May 1957, 45-47.

"Pincher Martin," *Radio Times*. 21 March 1958, 8.

"The Ladder and Tree," *Listener*. 24 March 1960, 531-33.

"Digging for Pictures," *Holiday*. March 1963, 86.

"Egypt and I," *Holiday*. April 1966, 32.

Foreword to Jack I. Biles, *Talk: Conversation with William Golding*. New York: Harcourt, 1970.

SECONDARY SOURCES

Books and Parts of Books

Babb, Howard S. *The Novels of William Golding*. Columbia: Ohio State University Press, 1973.

Baker, James R. *William Golding: A Critical Study*. New York: St. Martin's Press, 1965.

Baker, James R. and Arthur P. Ziegler, Fr. Eds. Casebook editor of *William Golding's Lord of the Flies*. New York: G.P.. Putnam's Sons, 1964.

Boyd, Stephen S.J. *The Novels of William Golding*. The Harvester Press Ltd., Harvester Wheatsheaf, 1988.

Biles, Jack I. and Evans, Robert C. (Eds.) *William Golding: Some Critical Considerations*. Lexington: The University Press of Kentucky, 1978.

———. *Talk: Conversations with William Golding*. New York: Harcourt, 1970.

Burgees, Anthony. *The Novel Now: A Guide to Contemporary Fiction*. New York: W.W. Norton & Co., Inc., 1967.

Carey, John. *William Golding, The Man and His Books: A Tribute on His 75th Birthday*. London: Faber and Faber, 1986.

Clark, George R. "In Illiberal Education: William Golding's Pedagogy." In whit-bread, Thomas B. ed., *Seven Contemporary Authors: Essays on Conzzens, Miller, West, Golding, Heller, Albee and Powers*. Austin: University of Texas Press, 1966, 73-93.

Dewsnap, Terence. *William Golding's Lord of the Flies* and *The Inheritors* 'Pincher Martin' 'Free Fall.' Monarch Literature Notes: New York, 1964.

Dick, Bernard F. *William Golding*. Twayne's English Authors Series, No. 57, New York: Twayne, 1967.

Elmen, Paul. *William Golding: A Critical Essay*. Contemporary Writers in Christian Perspective. Grand Rapids, Mich: Eerdmans, 1967.

Epstein, E.L. Notes on "Lord of the Flies" in *Lord of the Flies*. New York: Capricorn Books, 1959.

Erasmus, Desiderius. *Praise of Folly*, ed. A.H.T. Levi (Penui, Harmondsworth, 1971).

Forster, E.M. "Introduction" *Lord of the Flies*. New York: Coward McCann, 1962, IX-XII.

Fuller, Nicola C. Dicken. *William Golding's Use of Symbolism*. Britain, 1990.

Gindin, James. "'Gimmick' and Metaphor in the Novels of William Golding" in *Post-war British Fiction: New Accents and Attitudes*. Berkeley: University of California Press, 1962, 196-206.

Hudson, Leighton. *William Golding*. Writers and Critics, No. 61, Edinburgh: Oliver and Boyd Ltd., 1969.

Hynes, Samuel. *William Golding*. Columbia Essays on Modern Writers, 2nd edn. New York: Columbia University Press, 1968.

———. *Moral Models: William Golding's Novels: 1954-67*, ed. Norman Page, 1985.

Jackson, Frederick. *An outline of Lord of the Flies*. Toronto: Forum House, 1965.

Josipovici, Gabriel. *The World and the Book: A Study of Modern Fiction*, Macmillan, Bassingstoke & London, 1971.

Karl, Frederick R. *The Contemporary English Novel*. London: Thames and Hudson, 1964, 254-60.

Keene, Dennis. *William Golding and Jehovah*. Kyoto, Japan: University of Kyoto Press, 1963.

Kermode, Frank. *Puzzles and Epiphanies: Essays and Reviews* 1958-1961. London: Routledge and Kegan Paul, 1962.

Kinkead-Weekes, Mark and Ian Gregor. *William Golding: A Critical Study*. London: Faber and Faber, 1970.

Medcalf, Stephen. *William Golding*. Writers and their work No. 243, London: Longman, 1975.

Moody, Philippa. *Golding's Lord of the Flies: A Critical Commentary*. London: Macmillan's Press, 1966.

Nelson, W. (ed). *William Golding Lord of the Flies*. A Source Book, New York: The Odyssey Press, 1963.

Niven, Alastair, *Notes on Lord of the Flies*. New York: Longman, 1980.

Oldsey, Bernard S. and Stanley, Weintraub. *The Art of William Golding*. New York: Harcourt, Brace & World, Inc., 1965.

Page, Norman. *William Golding's Novels: 1954-67*, Casebook Series. London: Macmillan Education Ltd., 1985.

Pemberton, Oliver. *William Golding*. London: Longman Green, 1969.

Stern, J.P. *On Realism*. London: Routledge & Kegan Paul, 1973, 20-27, 131.

Talon, Henri A. "Le Mal dans l'oeuvre de William Golding: *Archives des Lettres Modernes*," 6 (1966), 1-88.

Tiger, Virginia. *William Golding: The Dark Fields of Discovery*. London: Calder & Boyars, 1974.

Webster, Owen, *Novelists in Interview*. New York, London: Metheum, 1985.

Walle, Louis J. *Out of Chaos*. Boston: Houghton Mufflin Company, 1977.

Whitley, John S. *Golding: Lord of the Flies*. Studies in English Literature, No. 42, ed. London: Edward Arnold, 1970.

Articles and Reviews

Adriaens, Mark. "Style in William Golding's The Inheritors." *English Studies,* 51 (February 1979), 16-30.

Alcantara-Dimalanta, O. "Christian Dimensions in Contemporary Literature." *Unitas*, 46, 1973, 213-23.

Allen, Water. "Recent Trends in the English Novel." *English*, 18 (Spring 1976), 2-5.

Anderson, Robert S. "Lord of the Flies on Coral Island." *Canadian Review of Sociology and Anthropology* (February 1967), 54-69.

Babb, James R. "The Decline of Lord of the Flies." *South Atlantic Quarterly*, 69 (Autumn 1970), 446-60.

———. "Why its No Go: A Study of William Golding's Lord of the Flies." *Arizona Quarterly*, 19 (Winter, 1963), 203-305.

———. "Literary Sources and William Golding". *South Atlantic Bulletin*, 37 (May 1972), 29-36.

Biles, Jack I. and Carl, R. Kropf. "The Cleft Rock of Conversion: Robinson Crusoe and Pincher Martin." *Studies in the Literary Imagination*, 2 (October 1969), 17-43.

Biles, Jack I. "A William Golding Miscellany." *Studies in the Literary Imagination*, II. George State College, pa, 1963.

Blake, Ian. "Pincher Martin: William Golding and 'Taffrail'." *Notes and Queries*, August 1962, 309-10.

Boyd, William. "Mariner and Albatross." *London Magazine*, 20 (February/March 1981), 89-94.

———. "Recent Novels." *Critical Survey*, 1 (Summer, 1964), 193-96.

Braybrooke, Neville. "The Return of Pincher Martin." *Commonweal*, 25 (October 1968), 115.

Burkin, E.C. "The Ironic Art of William Golding's the Inheritors." *Texas Studies in Literature and Language*, 9 (Winter 1968), 567-78.

———. "Lord of the Flies: An Analysis." *Georgia Review*, 19 (Spring 1965), 40-57.

Burgees, Anthony. "Golding Unbuttoned." *The Listener*, 4 (November 1965), 717-18.

———. "Religion and the Arts: 1—The Manicheans." *Times Literary Supplement*, 3 (March 1966), 153-54.

Burroway, Janet. "Resurrected Metaphor in The Inheritors." by William Golding, *Critical Quarterly*, 23 (Spring 1981), 53-70.

Capey, A.C. "Will and 'Idea' in 'Lord of the Flies'." *The Use of English*, 24 (Winter 1972), 99-107.

Cox, C.B. "Lord of the Flies." *Critical Quarterly*, 2 (Summer 1960), 112-17.

Davies, Douglas M. "Conversation with Golding." *New Republic*, 168 (May 4, 1963), 28-30.

Davies, Harold. "Moral Choice in the Novels of William Golding." *Moderna Sprak*, 11 (1969), 1.

Delbaere-Garant, Jeanne. "From the Cellar to the Rock: A Recurrent Pattern in William Golding's Novels." *Modern Fiction Studies*, 17 (1971-72), 501-12.

Dick, Bernard F. "The Novelist is a Displaced Person: An Interview with William Golding." *College English*, 26 (March 1965), 480-82.

Egan, John M. "Golding's View of Man." *America*, 26 (January 1963), 140-41.

Eller, Vernard. "Depravity or Sin." *Christian Charity*, 20 (November 1963), 1440.

Gindin, James. "Gimmick and Metaphor in the Novels of William Golding." *Modern Fiction Studies*, 6 (Summer 1960), 145-52.

Gordon, Robert C. "Classical Themes in Lord of the Flies." *Modern Fiction Studies*, 11 (Winter 1965-66), 424-27.

Green, Peter. "The World of the William Golding." *Review of English Literature*, 1 (April 1960), 62-72.

Golding to John Haffenden. "William Golding: An Interview." *Quarto Magazine*, Vol. 11, No. 12, November 1980.

Hynes, Samuel. "Novels of a Religious Man." *Commonweal*, 18 (March 1960), 673-75.

Kermode, Frank. "The Meaning of it All." *Books and Bookmen* (October 1959), pp. 9-10.

———. "The British Novel Lives." *Atlantic* (July 1972), 85-88.

———. "Coral Islands." *Spectator*, 22 (August 1958), 257.

Martin, Jerome. "Symbol Hunting: Golding's Lord of the Flies." *English Journal* (March 1969), 408-13.

Mitchell, Juliet. "Concept and Technique in William Golding." *New Left Review* (May-June 1962), 63-71.

Mitgang, Herbert. "William Golding's World." *New York Times Book Review*, 2 (November 1980), 47.

Muller, William R. "An Old Story Well Told: Commentary on William Golding's Lord of the Flies." *Christian Century*, 2 (October 1963), 1203-06.

Niemeyer, Carl. "The Coral Island Revisited." *College English* (January 1961), 241-45.

Oldsey, Bernard S. and Stanley, Weintraub. "'Lord of the Flies': Beelzebub Revisited." *College English*, XXV (November 1963), 90-99.

Pendry, E.D. "William Golding and 'Mankinds' Essential Illness." *Moderna Sprak*, 55 (1961), 4.

Pritchett, V.S. "God's Folly." *New Statesman*, 10 (April 1964), 562-63.

———. "Secret Parables." *New Statesman*, 2 (August 1958), 146-47.

Rexroth, Kenneth. "William Golding." *Atlantic Monthly*, 215 (May 1965), 96-98.

Rosenberg, Bruce A. "Lord of the Fire-Flies." *Centennial Review*, 11 (Winter 1967), 128-39.

Rosenfield, Claire. "Men of a Smaller Growth." A Psychological Analysis of William Golding's Lord of the Flies': *Literature and Psychology*, 11 (Autumn 1961), 93-101.

Ryan, J.S. "The Two Pincher Martin's: From Survival Adventures to Golding's Myth of Dying." *English Studies*, 55 (1974), 140-51.

Spitz, David. "Power and Authority: An Interpretation of Golding's Lord of the Flies." *Antioch Review*, 30 (Spring 1970), 21-33.

Stevens, Elizabeth. "Man is Born to Sin." *Books and Bookmen* (April 1964), 7-11.

Talon, Henri A. "Irony in 'Lord of the Flies.'" *Essays in Criticism*, 18 (July 1968), 296-309.

Taylor, Harry H. "The case against William Golding's Simon-Piggy." *Contemporary Review* (September 1966), 155-60.

Trilling, Lionel. "Lord of the Flies." *Mid-century* (October 1962), 10-12.

Walters, Margaret. "Two Fabulists: Golding and Camus." *Melbourne Critical Review*, 4 (1961), 18-29.

Watson, Kenneth. "A Reading of Lord of the Flies." *English*, 15 (Spring 1964), 2-7.

Webster, Owen. "Living and Chaos." *Books and Art* (March 1958), 15-16.

White, Robert, J. "Butterfly and Beast in 'Lord of the Flies'." *Modern Fiction Studies*, 10 (Summer 1964), 163-70.

Wilson, Angus. "Evil in the English Novel: Evil and the Novelist Today." *Listener*, 17 (January 1963), 115-17.

———. "Evil in the English Novel." *Books and Bookmen* (June 1963), 3.

Index

Allan, Walter, 18-19
Animal Farm, 14
Amis, Kingsley, 5
Auden, W.H., 35

Babb, Howard, 32
Baker, James R., 6, 12, 32, 52, 62, 139
Ballantyne, R.M., 7, 14, 34
Beckett, Samuel, 5
Benjamin, Walter, 139
Blake, 99
Boyle, Ted E., 46
Braine, John, 5
Brass Butterfly, The, 6
Bunyan, John, 14
Burgess, Anthony, 12, 17

Chesterton, G.K., 59
Churchill, Winston, 2
Close Quarters, 10
Coleridge, Samuel Taylor, 13
Conrad, Joseph, 15, 77
Connolly, Cyril, 124
Cooper, William, 5
Coral Island, The, 7, 14-15, 34-37, 53

Darkness Visible, 10-11, 18
Defoe, Daniel, 14, 16
Dorling, Taprell, 16
Durell, Lawrence, 5

Epstein, E.L., 32
Erasmus, 58

Fire Down Below, 10-11
Fleck, A.D., 19
Forster, E.M., 45
Free Fall, 8-9, 21, 109
Fromm, Erich, 106

Greene, Graham, 5, 123
Green, Peter, 16
Gregor, 120
Grisly Folk, The, 85
Gulliver's Travels, 14

Heart of Darkness, 15
Hewism, Robert, 5
High Wind in Jamaica, A, 15
Hotgate, The, 31, 33
Hugh, Richard, 15
Hueffer, Madox Ford, 77
Huxley, T.H., 3
Hynes, Samuel, 6, 114, 125

Inheritors, *The*, 7-8, 15, 21-22, 53, 76-121, 127-31, 133, 136-38, 142

Josipovici, Gabriel, 16, 109

Karl, Frederick, 33

Kermode, Frank, 13

Lord of the Flies, 7-8, 14-15, 21-22, 30-71, 81, 89, 94, 98, 100, 119, 127-32, 135, 137-38, 141

Lawry, Malcolm, 5

Master Builder, *The*, 9

Novel Now, The, 17

Oates, J.C., 130

Orwell, George, 5, 14

Osiris myth, 43

Outline of History, 76-77, 79-80, 85, 101

Paradise Lost, 9, 11, 14

Papermen, *The*, 10

Pilgrim's Progress, 14

Pincher Martin, 8, 15-16, 21-22, 128-30, 134, 136-37

Praise of Folly, 58

Prometheus Unbound, 16

Reader's Guide to The Contemporary English Novel, *A*, 33

Reik, Theodore, 105

Rexroth, Kenneth, 80-81

Rites of Passage, 10

Robinson Crusoe, 15, 17

Ryan, J.S., 77

Scorpion God, *The*, 21

Shakespeare, William, 17

Shelley, P.B., 16

Spender, Stephen, 123

Spire, *The*, 9, 21

Story of the Inner Life of the Royal Navy, *A*, 16

Strauss, Leo, 65

Swift, Jonathan, 14

Swiss Family Robinson, *The*, 15

Tiger, Virginia, 23, 139

Tillich, 126

Treasure Island, 31

Wain, John, 5

Waugh, Evelyn, 5, 14, 123

Webster, Owen, 18, 129

Weekes, Kinkead, 120

Wells, H.G., 7, 14, 37, 76, 85, 96, 101, 114, 124

Wind in the Willows, *The*, 31